MY HANDMADE WORLD

JO HANDMADE DESIGN / GIOVANNA MONFELI

METEOOR BOOKS

Hi!

I'm Giovanna, aka Jo, and I love to create treasures!

Be it graphic design, sewing, photography or carpentry, I like to work hard to make beautiful things. As a child I used to play with wood, nails and a hammer, dismantling toys and putting them back together. I also loved the workings of various crafts and memorized various techniques by carefully observing them, taking in all the steps. I particularly liked to observe the skilled hands of my grandmother, how fast and accurate they moved while sewing. I could watch her work for hours, enchanted by her skill, so I decided to learn the craft from scratch, and got started with a bunch of beautiful fabrics and my sewing machine.

I spent years trying to understand which craft suited me best. Slowly but surely, I realized that one single creative outlet was not enough for me. I realized that I could do anything I wanted, so I continued to experiment and refresh my creative passion. Thus, *Jo handmade design* was born, the proverbial treasure box containing all of my tools, ideas and projects.

Even more interesting than getting to work with my box, is showing its contents to fellow seamstresses. It's exciting to think that you're going to put these projects together as well, giving them your loving attention and personal style as you work along and add them to your very own treasure box.

This book is like a treasure map, opening to reveal 15 stylish designs. You can make them as home decorations or precious gifts for others to cherish. The sewing patterns include detailed instructions and step-by-step illustrations or photographs, and the large pattern sheets are included at the back.
Enjoy the book!

Jo

CONTENTS

BE PREPARED!

Gather your basic supplies and get ready to enter my (and soon also your) handmade world!

For every project you will need a **sewing machine**, **fabric scissors** and paper scissors, needles, pins and a **fabric pencil**. Keep your fabric scraps and leftovers close at hand: most projects allow you to go a bit wild with the **color combinations**! You can choose to make either a diverse ensemble or a well-balanced color composition, whatever suits your preference. The exact dimensions of the scraps and pieces of fabric needed are mentioned at the beginning of each pattern.

For several patterns (especially the ones using faux leather) you will need a piece of **cardboard** or **cardstock** to transfer your pattern onto the fabric.

In this book various kinds of **yarns**, **twines** and **threads** are used, we have illustrated them all.

Some of the patterns mention **fusible interfacing**, for a little reinforcement if the fabric of your choice is very thin. Products like Vlieseline H180 or H200, or Pellon SF101 Shape-Flex will do the trick. Woven fusible interfacing works fine too.

IT'S ALL ABOUT SHAPE

This book contains 15 sewing patterns, but several of them could also be called 'fabric sculpture patterns'. Since these patterns get the right shape the moment you stuff them, we have included some notes to keep in mind when choosing your supplies.

1 Don't make an arbitrary **choice of fabric** for the designs, but take a close look at the suggestions each pattern provides. I sometimes suggest solid fabrics because thin fabrics made the end result too fluffy. You might go wild and try out crazy materials, but if you do, try to sew a few 'fillable' test objects first, and always choose a material of comparable firmness.

2 Choose a straight stitch and a standard of slightly shorter **stitch length**, to make sure the stuffing will not pop out of the seam. For the same reason, being picky in your choice of **yarn color** is not a crime. When firmly stuffed, the seam will come under tension and the stitches will be visible, which is why backstitching and **securing the thread** are also very important.

THIN COTTON YARN

HEMP TWINE

STRONG COTTON YARN

TOPSTITCH THREAD

KITCHEN TWINE

THREAD

NYLON THREAD

WAXED THREAD

3 When we talk about getting 'in shape', the number one topics are usually diets and fitness. In My Handmade World, getting in shape is all about stuffing! Don't be thrifty on polyfill stuffing: it would be a pity to make a nicely sewn object and making it look a bit limpy by not **stuffing** it firmly. Start with the small parts. Use little balls of stuffing and press them firmly into every corner and crease. Don't use any sharp materials, and knead the parts while filling to spread it evenly.

4 Neatly sewn **curved seams** give the objects the right shape too. Use a shorter stitch length, about half of the regular stitch length. With concave (or inward) seams, you have to release the tension on the seam before you will be able to turn it. That's why you will need to clip the seam allowance. With convex (or outward) seams you will find that the seam allowance bunches up because there's too much fabric. Notching the seam allowance helps to remove the excess fabric. Clip or notch close to the stitching, but not closer than 1/46" (2 mm), so as not to accidently clip into your stitches. Same story for the corners: with outward corners, trim away the corner to reduce bulk in the seam allowance.

SEAM ALLOWANCE

Sewing with the right seam allowance is very important for the designs in this book: in order to make these projects a success, **make sure you meticulously sew at the indicated distance**. This seems obvious, but it might need some extra attention if you use the metric system (mm).
If there are inches marked on your sewing machine, it's quite easy: just use the seam allowance indicated, e.g. 1/4". If your sewing machine only has cm on it,

make sure you use 6 mm and do not round off to 5 mm. For the hot air balloon on p. 23 for example, you have to sew 16 segments together to make a balloon. With a surplus of 3/32" (2 mm) at each seam, you will end up with 1 1/4" (3.2 cm) in circumference, so the balloon won't fit the base. If you have a mm-only machine, decrease the seam allowance of your paper pattern pieces with 1 mm, or move your needle 1 mm to make sure you sew at 6 mm. Or simply mark the 6 mm measure on your machine with a pen or a piece of paper tape.

SKILL LEVELS

The skill level of each pattern is indicated as such:
● ○ ○   easy
● ● ○   intermediate
● ● ●   advanced

PATTERN STRUCTURE

These tips will help you navigate the book with ease.

This symbol refers to the pattern sheet. The pattern pieces are drawn either in red, blue or green (corresponding to the color of the symbol) and have a number (e.g. 1a) as well as a name (e.g. nose).

Next to the symbol for the pattern sheet you will find small representations of the pattern pieces that belong to this pattern, this will help you collect all the pieces you need from the sheet.

The steps that are accompanied by an illustration, picture or both are preceded by a colored number (e.g. 1), the other steps are preceded by a black number (e.g. **8**).

SOME TECHNIQUES

RUNNING STITCH

The running stitch is the basic stitch in sewing by hand and embroidery. The stitch is worked by passing the needle in and out of the fabric. Running stitches may be of varying length, depending on the use.

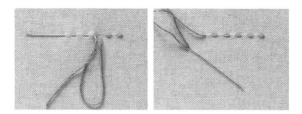

STEM STITCH

The stem stitch is an embroidery stitch used to form a continuous line, made by overlapping stitches. Each stitch is made backward to the general direction of sewing. Bring out your needle at the first point. Take it in through a second point, and bring it back out on a point right in between the first and the second point. As you progress, you will obtain a continuous line.

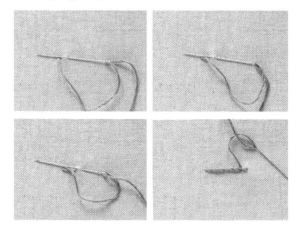

INVISIBLE STITCH OR LADDER STITCH

The invisible stitch is a hand stitch used to close openings, for example of stuffed items. It's a neat way to finish your project, because the stitches are nearly invisible! Thread your needle with thread that matches the color of the fabric. Hide the knot in the folded crease of the seam. Make sure the two folded edges are evenly aligned. Run the needle in the fold of the fabric and come out about 1/8" (3 mm) down along the fold. Insert the needle in the opposite fold and run it down the fold, again at about 1/8" (3 mm). As you continue going back and forth, pull the thread every few stitches to make an even and neat seam. When you reach the end of the opening, pull the thread tight. Knot off the thread and cut the excess.

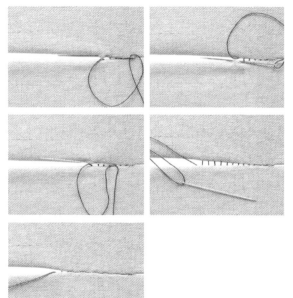

MIND THE LITTLE ONES

You don't need to be young to deserve a little cuteness sometimes, or decorate your home with a bit of a twist, but since I designed a couple of soft toys and balloons that make a perfect nursery mobile, we'll need to pay attention to **toy safety** as well.

If you decorate your nursery with one (or several) of the balloons, make sure the child cannot grab it, since the yarn is not strong enough to win a fight from exploring little hands (unaware of their own strength). If you make objects with small parts for a child, like a rabbit with eyes or a cat with whiskers, make sure you carefully secure the protruding parts.

You'll probably be familiar with some of the basic sewing techniques (like sewing parts right sides together), but working with faux leather might be a new experience for you. Try to find a piece of faux leather that is matt, soft to the touch and non-stretchable.

THREAD COLOR

It's important to choose a matching color for the thread, both for normal seams and topstitching. The material is stiffer then fabric, so the thread will always be visible in the seams.

PAPER PATTERN

The process of transferring the pattern and cutting the pieces is similar for all faux leather patterns. I myself prefer not to trace faux leather patterns by hand. There are a lot of exact points to transfer. Drawing them only approximately will not give you a satisfying end result. You could photocopy and glue the pattern pieces on a piece of cardstock, to make it easier to trace each shape on the faux leather. Or if you decide to trace by hand, use a thin sharpie and take your time.

TRANSFERRING LINES AND DOTS

Carefully cut out all the pieces of cardstock along the perimeter. Place them on the right side of the faux leather. Insert some paper tape between the cardstock and the faux leather pieces to fix them together. Check first to make sure the tape doesn't damage the material. Take a large embroidery needle with a pointed end or a stitching awl, and transfer all the dots illustrated on the pattern piece onto the faux leather. Put a piece of cardstock or other suitable material under the faux leather to avoid damaging the table top and needle tip. The transferred points on the faux leather will help you to make perfect seams. Test the faux leather of your choice, to see if the dots remain visible on its surface. Trace the outline of all parts of the pattern on the faux leather with a pen.

CUTTING

Remove the cardstock shapes and cut out each piece drawn on the faux leather exactly along the inside of the traced outline. In this way, completely removing the pen mark, you will get shapes identical to the pattern pieces.

FILLING

Projects like the hedgehog doorstop (p. 69) or the polar bear paper weight (p. 47) are filled with sand to make them stand up. If your faux leather is stiff, you can use coarse sand. If your faux leather is thin and soft (which I would recommend), choose fine-grained sand to make sure the shape of the grains isn't visible through the material. Pouring the sand directly into the faux leather would make the design apply for a subscription to daily vacuuming. That's why you have to insert a plastic bag first. Pour the sand into the bag, little by little, making sure everything is firmly filled. Repeatedly pierce the sand with a thin blunt-end stick to fill any empty spaces. Fill the container almost to the top: the sand should be firmly pressed together.

FLYING RABBIT

The rabbit is 15 1/2" (39.5 cm) long and 4 6/8" (12 cm) wide.

● ● ○

- -

WHAT YOU'LL NEED

- polyfill stuffing
- colored cotton thread
- plain or printed cotton fabric:
    3 1/8" x 4" (8 x 10 cm) for the nose
    6" x 6" (15 x 15 cm) for the front of the ears
- pile or soft fabric:
    14 1/2" x 19 1/2" (37 x 50 cm) for the belly,
        head, back ears and tail
- wool or cotton fabric:
    7" x 18" (18 x 45 cm) for the back of the body
        and the forepaws
- cardstock

OPTIONAL

- tweezers (to stuff the tail of the rabbit with polyfill
    stuffing, see step 24)

CUTTING AND PREPARING THE MATERIAL

Read through the instructions before starting. Seam allowances are included in all pattern pieces where applicable. Draw the reference marks shown on the pattern on the wrong side of each piece.

1. Trace the **nose** (**1a**) on the wrong side of a piece of cotton fabric. Cut out the nose with a 1/4" (6 mm) seam allowance, as shown by the dotted line on the pattern piece.

2. Trace two **front ears** (**1b**) on the wrong side of a piece of cotton fabric. Cut out the ears with a 1/4" (6 mm) seam allowance and 1/2" (12 mm) on the bottom side, as shown by the dotted line on the pattern piece.

3. Trace two **back ears** (**1c**), the **belly** (**1d**), the two sides (upper and bottom) of the **head** (**1e**) and the **tail** (**1f**) onto the wrong side of the pile. Cut out the pieces with a 1/4" (6 mm) seam allowance as shown by the dotted line on the pattern piece. Leave a 1/2" (12 mm) seam allowance at the bottom of the back ears and leave no seam allowance around the tail.

4. Trace the **back body** (**1g**) and the **forepaws** (**1h**) onto the wrong side of the wool fabric. Cut out the pieces with a 1/4" (6 mm) seam allowance, as shown by the dotted line on the pattern piece.

5. Trace the shapes **nose** (**1i**) and **body** (**1j**) onto a piece of cardstock and cut them.

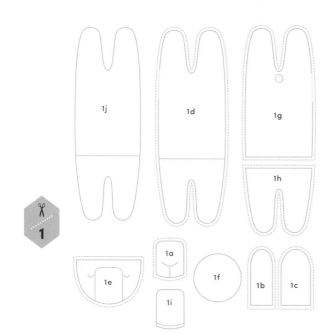

1j

1d

1g

1h

1

1e

1a

1i

1f

1b

1c

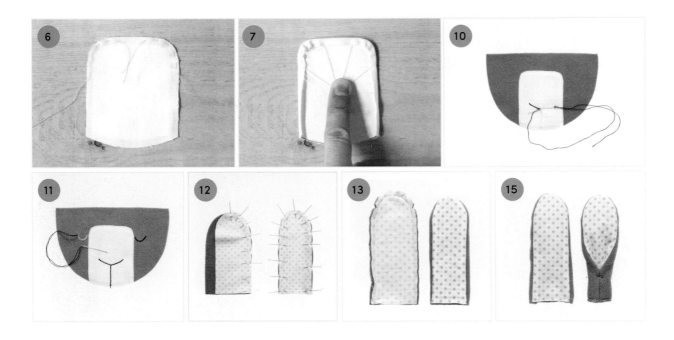

NOSE

6. Sew a running stitch* along the two curved portions of the perimeter of the nose (**1a**) by hand, as shown in the picture. Insert the cardstock shape (**1i**) on the wrong side into the fabric.

7. Pull the two ends of the threads. Iron the folded edge over the paper piece all around the nose and remove the cardstock.

8. Draw the lines of the nose with a crayon on the right side of the fabric.

9. Put the nose piece on top of the upper head and pin it in place. The right side of the fabrics faces up. Topstitch close to the folded edge of the nose.

10. Embroider the lines of the nose with a colored cotton thread.

11. Trace the eyes on the head at the sides of the nose and embroider them with a black or your preferred color cotton thread, as shown in the picture. Secure the loose ends on the wrong side of the fabric.

EARS

12. Place the front and back ear pieces with right sides together. Match and pin the ears along the edges, as shown in the picture.

13. Sew all around the ears at 1/4" (6 mm) of seam allowance from the edge, but leave the bottom side open. Notch the curved edge and turn the ears right side out.

14. Stuff only the top half of the ears with polyfill stuffing.

15. Stitch the open side near the edge. Fold the right and left sides of the ears towards the center, as shown in the picture. Lock the edges with a seam at the bottom and with a pin a bit higher, at about 1" (2.5 cm).

---

* see p. 10

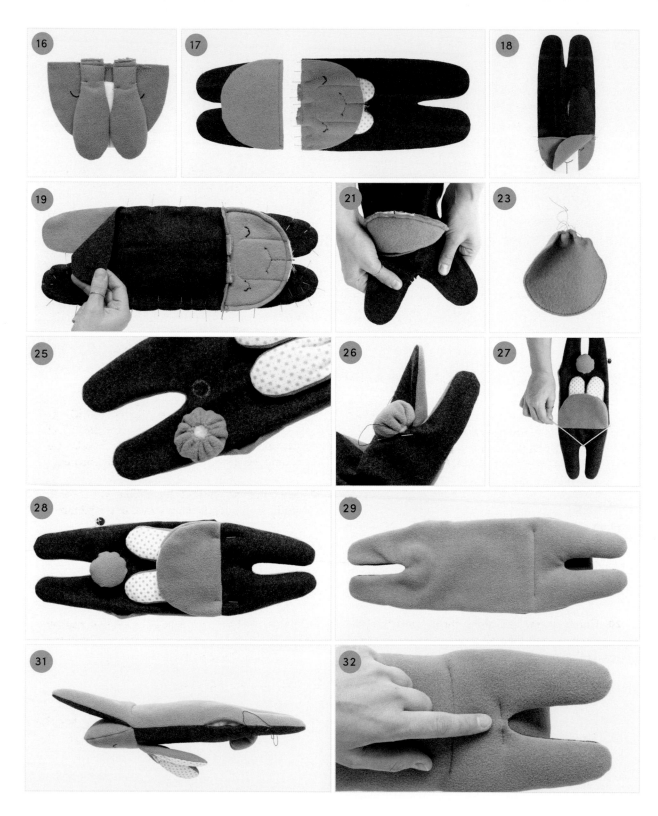

HEAD

16. Pin the ears over the upper head, as shown in the picture. Each ear is at 1/4" (6 mm) from the center of the head and extends 1/4" (6 mm) from the top of it. Sew the pieces together along and near the head top edge.

17. Place the upper head on top of the back body (**1g**) and the bottom head on top of the forepaws (**1h**), right sides together, by matching the AB line. Pin and sew both pieces at 1/4" (6 mm) from the edge.

Note

The seams must follow the full line drawn on the pattern piece exactly from point A to B. Do not sew through the seam allowance up to the raw edge.
----

18. Unfold and match the two pieces of the upper and bottom head you've just sewn and place them on top of each other, right sides together. Pin and sew the round edge of the upper and bottom head, using a seam allowance of 1/4" (6 mm), and sew exactly from point A to B.

BODY

19. Keeping the head wrong side out, unfold the forepaws of the piece you've just sewn. Place it on top of the belly (**1d**) by matching the AB line, right sides together. Pin all around the back body and the forepaws with the belly piece.

20. Carefully sew first along the perimeter of the forepaws and then all around the back body, at 1/4" (6 mm) from the edge. Leave a section of the perimeter open, as shown in the pattern, so you can turn the rabbit right side out later on. Always sew from point A to point B, no further than this.

   To make it easier to follow the seam line between the legs of the rabbit, you can use the body shape (**1j**) to mark it on the wrong side of the fabric.

21. Clip the seam allowance between the paws of the rabbit and notch the curved edge. You can jump the second step if the fabric you've chosen is very soft, as it is in my case.

22. Turn the rabbit right side out. First do the ears and the head, then the paws and the body.

23. Do a running stitch around the tail or sew around by machine on the longest stitch length, setting the thread tension at the minimum, without securing the thread at the beginning and at the end. Pull the running stitch to make the fabric curl, and make sure the right side of the fabric is on the outside. Tie the threads and cut the ends.

24. Stuff the tail with a bit of polyfill stuffing, using tweezers or a small stick.

25/26.
   Place the tail on the back of the rabbit, with the hole toward the contact point. Sew the tail at the back body by hand, all around the hole. Tie the thread inside the body and cut the surplus.

27. Stuff the forepaws of the rabbit with polyfill stuffing up until the lines shown in the picture.

28/29.
   Pin and close the forepaws along the AB line. Leave 1" (2,5 cm) on both sides of the seam, as shown in the pictures.

30. Stuff the rabbit with small amounts of polyfill stuffing at a time. Start with the head and the rear paws, then stuff the body.

31. Sew the opening by hand.

32. Pin and sew the center point of the forepaws at the bottom head piece by hand.

STAR PILLOW

The radius of the star is about 11" (28 cm).

● ○ ○

WHAT YOU'LL NEED

- polyfill stuffing
- wooden skewer (for turning)
- cardstock
- plain and printed cotton fabric:
    5 pieces of 8" x 12" (20 x 30 cm) for the
      front of the star
    21" x 21" (53 x 53 cm) for the back of the star
    2 pieces of 9" x 5 1/2" (23 x 14 cm) for the nodes

OPTIONAL

- fusible interfacing (as reinforcement if the fabric
  of your choice is very thin)

CUTTING AND PREPARING THE MATERIAL

Read through the instructions before starting. Seam allowances are included in all pattern pieces where applicable.

1. Put the two rectangles of the fabric you've chosen for the nodes on top of each other, right sides together. Trace five **nodes (2a)** onto the wrong side of one piece of fabric, with a distance of about 3/8" (10 mm) between each node. Pin the fabric layers together.

2. Trace five patterns of the **tip** (**2b**) onto the wrong side of each rectangle of fabric you've chosen for the front of the pillow and transfer the marks. If you want to make a star with a seamless front, follow the steps for the back of the pillow. Cut out all the pieces with a 1/4" (6 mm) seam allowance, as shown by the dotted line on the pattern piece.

3. Trace the whole star onto the wrong side of the fabric you've chosen for the back of the pillow. Rotate the pattern piece **tip** (**2c**) around the center of the fabric square and mark the perimeter each time. Cut out the full star with a 1/4" (6 mm) seam allowance, as shown by the dotted line on the pattern piece.

4. Trace and cut the **tip shape** (**2d**) onto a piece of cardstock.

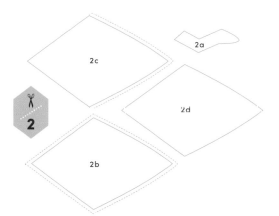

NODES

5. Sew along the perimeter of the nodes. Leave the side AB indicated on the pattern piece open, so you can turn the nodes right side out later on. Cut the nodes with a seam allowance of 1/8" (3 mm), but cut the open side without seam allowance.

6. Cut the tips and clip the corners. Be very careful not to cut the seam.

7. Turn the nodes right side out. Use a wooden skewer to gently push the fabric through the opening.

FRONT OF THE STAR

8. Choose the sequence of the fabrics and sew the adjacent edges of the tips. Put the shapes two by two on top of each other, right sides together, and sew them together on the exact line from point C to D, as indicated on the pattern piece. Make sure you don't sew through the seam allowance up to the raw edge.

9. Press the seam allowances open.

PUT ALL THE PIECES TOGETHER

10/11.

Pin a node in each tip of the back of the star between the marks drawn on the pattern piece, as shown in the pictures. Fold and pin each node to the fabric of the back side, to make sure you don't catch the rest of the nodes when you sew the front and the back of the star together. Put the front and the back sides of the star on top of each other, right sides together. Close the tips and secure the fabric with a couple of pins.

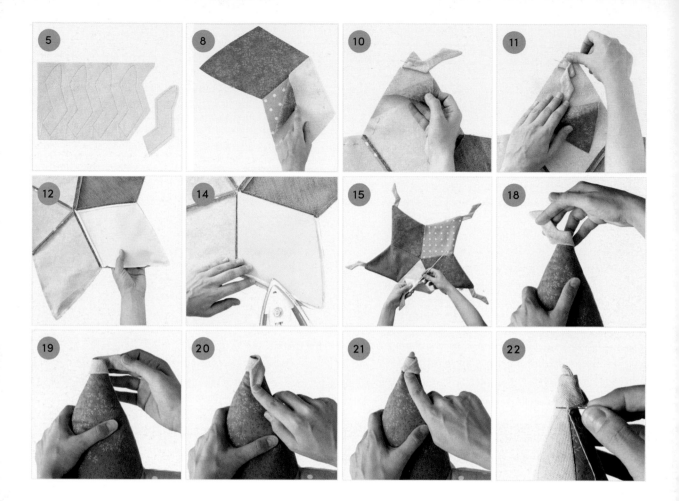

12. Carefully sew the star all around, using a seam allowance of 1/4" (6 mm). Leave open a section of the perimeter that is big enough to insert your hand.

13. Cut the tips and clip the corners along the seam allowance. Be careful not to cut the seam.

14. Press the edges of the section left open, as shown in the picture. To fold them, use the tip shape of cardstock. Fold the seam allowance over the cardstock and press with the iron. Do one side first, and then the other.

15. Turn the star right side out. Use a wooden skewer to gently push the tips out.

16. Stuff the pillow with small amounts of polyfill stuffing at a time. First fill the tips and then the center of the star.

17. Sew the opening by hand.

18/19/20/21.
Wrap each node around the tips of the star, as shown in the pictures. Tuck the tip of the node underneath, like if you would make a knot.

22. Sew the free corner of the node to the side of the star tip by hand.

"All my designs are born out of the desire to create something beautiful for the little ones, made with love and high-quality materials. It's important to grow up surrounded by softness, comfort, trust and inspiration to play and develop your own imagination. This really is a life-long project, so I love to make grown-ups play and daydream too. The star pillow, for example, is about imagination. I love stars and the way they light up dark moments. The knotted tips are my way to dream about how it would be if I could catch a star and anchor it to the world to embrace it whenever I needed it."

BIG HOT AIR BALLOON WITH BASKET, FLAGS, STARS AND CLOUDS

The hot air balloon measures 7 7/8" (20 cm) in diameter.

●●●

- -

WHAT YOU'LL NEED

- fabric glue
- polyfill stuffing
- wooden skewer (for turning)
- 2 clothespins
- kitchen twine or strong cotton yarn
- thin cotton yarn
- colored cotton thread
- cardstock
- 1/8" (3 mm) thick felt
    7 3/8" x 6" (18.5 x 15 cm)
- plain and printed cotton fabric:
    4 pieces of 9 3/8" x 13 7/8" (24 x 35 cm) in
        different fabrics for the balloon
    8 7/8" x 6 3/8" (22 x 16 cm) for the top and
        the base of the balloon
    15 x 6 3/8" (38 x 16 cm) for the basket
    12 2/8" x 7" (31 x 18 cm) for flags and weights
    2 pieces of 8 7/8" x 6 1/8" (22 x 15.5 cm) in
        different fabrics for the stars
    2 pieces of 13" x 3 6/8" (33 x 9 cm) in different
        fabrics for the clouds

OPTIONAL

- fusible interfacing (as reinforcement if the fabric
  of your choice is very thin)
- fabric hole punch (to make holes in 3 mm thick felt,
  see step 22)
- tweezers (to stuff the stars and clouds with polyfill
  stuffing, see step 42)

CUTTING AND PREPARING THE FABRIC

Read through the instructions before starting. Seam
allowances are included in all pattern pieces where
applicable.

1. Trace four pieces of **segment (3a)** on the wrong
    side of each of the four different fabrics chosen
    for the balloon. Cut out the sixteen pieces with
    a 1/4" (6 mm) seam allowance, as shown by the
    dotted line in the pattern.
    Trace the **base ring (3b)**, the **base circle (3c)**
    and the **top circle (3d)** of the hot air balloon
    onto the wrong side of the fifth fabric. Cut out all
    the pieces with a 1/4" (6 mm) seam allowance as
    indicated on the pattern by the dotted line.
    Trace four **basket sides (3e)**, one **bottom
    base (3f)** and one **top base (3g)** onto the wrong
    side of the fabric you've chosen for the basket.
    Cut out all the pieces (except for the top base)
    with a 1/4" (6 mm) seam allowance as indicated
    on the pattern by the dotted line.

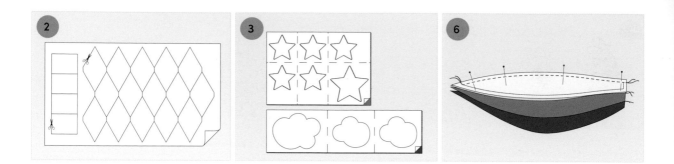

BALLOON

2. Trace four **weight bags** (**3h**) and fifteen **flags** (**3i**) onto the wrong side of the fabric. Cut out all the pieces without a seam allowance.

3. Put the two fabrics you've chosen for the stars and clouds on top of each other, right sides together. Trace the shapes of five **little stars** (**3j**), one **big star** (**3k**), two **little clouds** (**3l**) and one **big cloud** (**3m**) onto the wrong side of one piece of cotton fabric, as shown in the figure.

4. Trace one **reinforcement** (**3n**), the **supports** (**3o**) and (**3p**), and the **basket bases** (**3q**) and (**3r**) on a piece of 3 mm thick felt. Cut them without seam allowance.

5. Trace and cut onto a piece of cardstock the shapes **top circle** (**3s**), **little cloud** (**3t**) and **big cloud** (**3u**).

6. Choose the sequence of the fabrics according to the color, for example three shades of blue and then cream, repeated four times. Put the segments two by two on top of each other, right sides together, and sew them as shown in the figure.

Important: The seams of the segments must follow the full lines drawn on the pattern piece as precisely as possible, so that the balloon will perfectly match the base. Do not sew through the seam allowance up to the raw edge, but start from the x-point at the top of each segment.

Combine eight segments at a time to make the two halves of the balloon.

7. To give the balloon a perfect shape, press the seam allowances between the segments open. Press as you go.

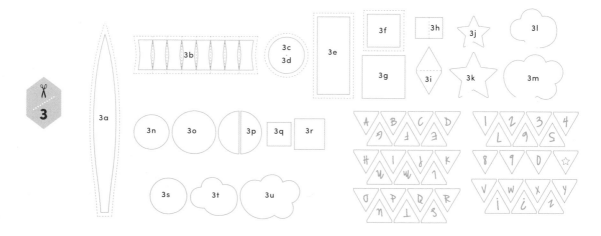

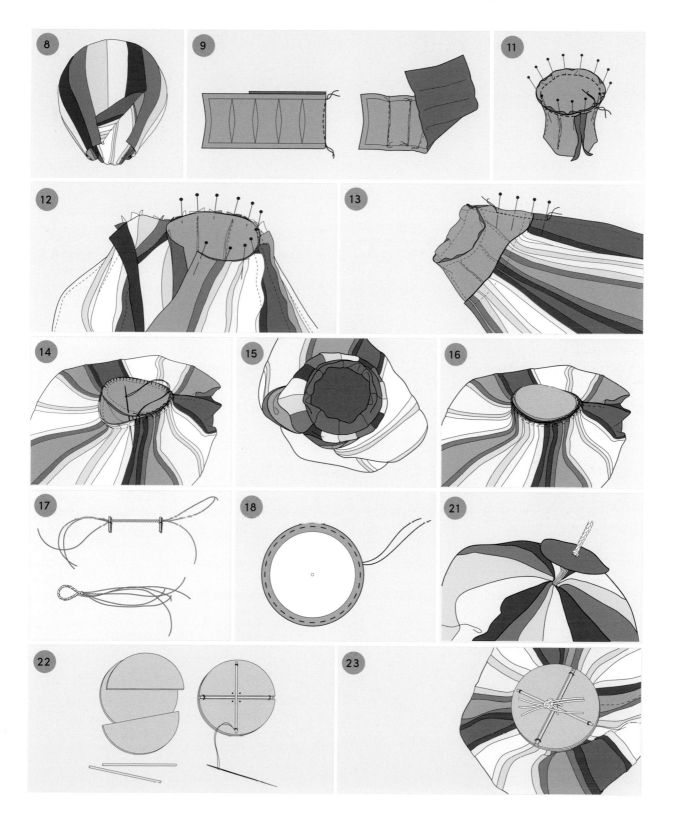

8. Put the two halves of the balloon on top of each other, right sides together. Pin carefully and sew them, leaving an opening of 5" (13 cm) on one side, as shown in the figure.

BASE OF THE BALLOON

9. Sew the darts of the base ring one by one. Fold the strip of fabric in half on the folding line, right sides together, and sew following the sewing line, as shown in the figure. Be careful not to sew through the seam allowance.

10. Close the base ring: fold the strip of fabric in half, right sides together, and sew half of the short side.

11. Put the base ring with the partly opened side seam downwards. Pin the circle (**3c**) together with the open top of the base ring, right sides together. Sew with a seam allowance of 1/4" (6 mm). Turn the piece inside out.

12. Insert the base ring inside the balloon, right sides together. Pin the top of the ring to the bottom of the balloon. Start at the opening in the side seam of both balloon and base. Align each crease of the base ring with the seams at every two color segments of the balloon, as shown in the figure. Carefully sew them together, using a seam allowance of 1/4" (6 mm).

13. Push the base of the balloon inside out. Pin and sew the open side of the base ring and 1" (2.5 cm) of the open side of the balloon. Keep the seam allowance between the ring and the balloon folded upward, in the direction of the balloon while sewing.

14. Push the base ring inside the balloon until the seam allowance of the base circle is level with the opening in the balloon. Position the raw edges of the top and the base circle together (the base ring is now folded in half, wrong sides together). Join the raw edges of the top and bottom of the base ring and sew them together to the balloon, as shown in the figure.

15. In this way, the base ring of the balloon – seen in the figure from the right side of the work – creates an edge that is deep enough to simulate the vacuum inside of a real hot air balloon.

REINFORCEMENT AT THE BASE OF THE BALLOON

16. Glue the felt reinforcement (**3n**) to the base, on the wrong side of the fabric circle. This will help shape the hot air balloon, as well as give more stability to the bottom of the balloon. Glue the seam allowance all around the piece of felt. Instead of gluing, you could also sew the circle by hand at the seam allowance of the bottom of the balloon, but glue will make your balloon sturdier.

TOP OF THE BALLOON

17. Cut three 16" (40 cm) pieces of kitchen twine to make the loop. Lock the pieces together with a clothespin on 3 7/8" (10 cm) from one end, make a braid of 3 1/8" (8 cm) and lock with a clothespin, leaving another 3 7/8" (10 cm) unbraided at the end. Fold the braid in half and knot the ends together.

18. To finish the top of the balloon, use a basting stitch along the perimeter of the top circle (**3d**) and insert the cardstock shape (**3s**) on the wrong side into the fabric. Pull and tie the two ends of the thread.

Note

Lacing can be done by hand, but you can also use the longest stitch length of your sewing machine, setting the thread tension at the minimum. Leave a long tail of thread at the beginning, sew all around the circle without backstitching neither at the start nor at the end, and leave a long tail at the end as well.

19. Iron the folded edge and remove the cardstock.

20. Pierce the center of the top circle (**3d**) with a large needle and pass the ends of the twine hook one by one inside it.

21. Turn the balloon right side out. Insert the ends of the twine at the center top of the balloon, between the outer tips of the segments.

22. Take the two big circles of felt. Put felt support (**3p**) on top of felt support (**3o**) by matching the shapes. Take a wooden skewer and cut it into two sticks of 2 7/8" (7.3 cm) each. Insert one stick between the two parts of felt support (**3p**) and put the other stick on top to form a cross shape. Lock the sticks into place with some small stitches at the four ends of the sticks. Use a fabric hole punch or large needle to make four holes in the felt, right next to the intersection of the sticks.

23. Turn the balloon inside out. Use a large needle to pass the twine ends through the four holes in the felt. Securely tie the twine ends above the intersection of the sticks, as shown in the figure. This method is really safe and makes sure the form of the hot air balloon will not change when you hang it. Turn the balloon right side out again.

BASKET

24. Put the sides of the basket (**3e**) two by two on top of each other, right sides together, and sew them as shown in the figure. Combine all four rectangles to make a tube. Press the seam allowances open.

25. Fold the tube, wrong sides together: align the raw edges of the top and bottom of the tube. Pin one side of the bottom base (**3f**) to the open edges of the tube, right side facing inward. Pay attention to the position of the seams in the tube: the center of the side base must correspond to the vertical seams of the basket.

26. Sew the first side of the basket. Stop the machine in the corner, with the needle still in the fabric, and turn the basket 90°. Pin the second side base on the corresponding edge of the tube and sew until you reach the next corner. Continue in the same way until you reach the end of the tube.

27. Clip the seam allowances on the corners of the base. Be very careful not to cut the seam. Turn the basket right side out.

28. To fill the empty space between the seam allowances in the basket, glue felt piece (**3q**) on the inside.

29. Glue felt piece (**3r**) in the center of the top base (**3g**) piece, on the wrong side. Cut the corners as shown in the figure. Fold and glue the edges of the fabric square onto the felt. Pay attention to the corners.

30. Glue the top base inside the basket. Press well onto felt piece (**3q**) and the seam allowances. Fold the edge of the basket slightly outward (about 3/8" - 10 mm).

31. Use a thin cotton yarn to connect the basket to the base of the hot air balloon. Pass a needle under the edge to tie one end of the cotton yarn to a corner of the basket. Insert the needle into the fold of the ring you made in step 30, and pass along one crease until you reach the inside of the balloon. Adjust the length of the yarn so that the basket hangs about 2 6/8" (7 cm) under the balloon. Lock the yarn inside the balloon. Do this for all four top corners of the basket.

WEIGHT BAGS

32. Fold the rectangle for the weight bag in half on the folding line, right sides together. Sew at 1/8" (3 mm) from the edge.

33. Open the seam with your fingers and push it down in the center of the tube as shown in the figure. Sew one of the short sides of the bag at 1/8" (3 mm) from the edge.

34. Turn the little bag right side out. Fold the open edge inward for 3/8" (10 mm).

35. Use a basting stitch all around the opening of the bag, at 1 5/8" (5 mm) from the top edge. Start and finish on the back, corresponding with the vertical seam.

36. Stuff the little bag and pull the threads around the opening. Turn the threads a couple of times around the neck of the bag and tie them at the back. Sew the weights to the four corners of the basket by hand, just below the basket's edge.

STARS, CLOUDS AND FLAGS

37. Cut out separate squares of fabric for each star and cloud. Pin the fabric layers together and sew carefully along the lines. Sew by machine or by hand with small stitches. Leave a section of the perimeter open, so you can turn the stars and the clouds right side out later on.

38. Cut out the stars, leaving a 1/8" (3 mm) seam allowance (the seam allowance can be a little wider in the open area) and cut the tips and corners. Be very careful not to cut the seam. Cut out the clouds, leaving a 1 5/8" (5 mm) seam allowance and cut the corners.

39. Use the iron to fold the open seam allowance on each star, as shown in the figure. This simple trick will make it easier to close the opening once the star is turned right side out.

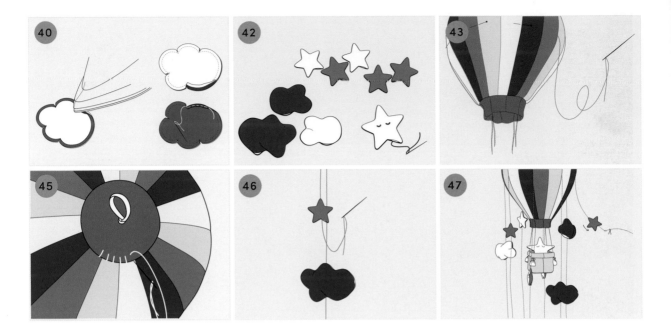

40. Pressing the seam allowance of the clouds makes it easier to close them. As this seam is curved, you can use a cardstock template to help you with the ironing. Take the cloud templates (**3t**) and (**3u**) to easily bend the curved seam allowances. Put a fabric cloud on the ironing board and put the corresponding template on top, matching the design. Fold the open seam allowance of the cloud over the cardstock, pressing with the tip of the iron. Iron the sides one after another. If necessary, lock the edges you have ironed into place with a couple of basting stitches.

41. Turn the stars and clouds right side out. Push the fabric gently through the opening with a skewer. Be particularly careful with the little stars. Draw the eyes on the big star and embroider them with a cotton or topstitching thread.

42. Stuff all the stars and clouds. For the parts that are most difficult to reach, you can use tweezers to take very small amounts of stuffing and push them inside the shape with a skewer. Sew the opening of the big star by hand.

43. Now take the balloon and mark it with pins at every two segments and at 6" (15 cm) from the center top. Pass eight cotton threads of 16-20" (40-50 cm) long through the points you've marked to hang the stars and clouds. Pass through the opening in the balloon to fix each cotton thread inside.

44. Stuff the balloon by pressing the stuffing inside. The balloon must be taut and firm. Close the opening by hand, between the segments.

45. Sew the fabric top circle with a cotton or top-stitching thread.

46. Hang the hot air balloon. Attach the little stars and clouds to the cotton threads all around the balloon. Pass the thread inside the stars with a needle. Enter at the upper tip and out from the opening at the bottom. Do the same thing for the clouds, but enter at the center top point where the weight of the clouds is well-balanced.

47. Slide the small stars and clouds along the threads to find a balanced composition. You can then lock them in the chosen position. Measure the length between the balloon and for example the tip of one star. Slide up the star and tie a knot in the thread at the distance you've measured. Then slide the star down again until you reach the

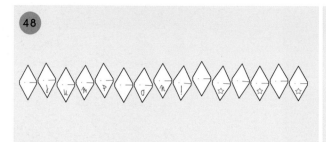

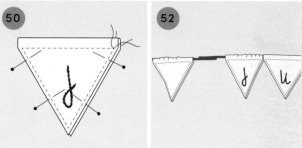

knot, cut the surplus thread and hide it inside the star. Once you have fixed all the elements, you can remove the balloon from the hook and sew the openings of the stars and clouds by hand. If the fabric is a little crumpled in the end, you can iron it, but without applying pressure. Stuff a little bit of stuffing into the basket and put the big star to sleep inside it.

48. Line up the fifteen flags. Choose what to write on them and how to fill the spaces between the beginning and the end of the words, as shown in the figure.

49. Draw the letters and symbols you've chosen onto the flags with a pencil. Embroider them with colored cotton thread using a stem stitch* or another stitch of your choice.

50. Fold the flags in half, wrong sides together, and sew the tips very close to the edges. The top side must be sewn at a distance of 1/8" (3 mm) from the edge, so a piece of twine can pass through.

51. Pass a 26" (66 cm) piece of twine through all the flags in the selected order. If you use a soft cotton thread instead, use a darning needle to pass the thread through the flags.

52. When the row of flags is finished, it must measure 25" (63.5 cm), corresponding to the circumference of the balloon. To close the loop, pull the flags a little inward, put both ends of the twine on top of each other (1" - 2.5 cm at each end) and glue them together. Loosen the flags again to hide the twine. Put the flags around the balloon.

*see p. 10

" *I buy most of my fabrics in two or three shops around the corner. I like to see the textures, colors and prints of the materials and touch them to see if they are suitable for my projects. I love simple color palettes in delicate tones. I always start from a neutral color and add one or maximum two dominant colors, inspired by photography or nature. A combination of colors that are too bright or excessive can easily overrule the form of the design. I'd love to draw custom graphics and print them on fabric: it would make my projects complete. Recycled fabrics are fun to work with too: the denim I used in the big hot air balloon, for example, had a former life as a garment, and the base ring is the cuff of an old shirt.*"

HEDGEHOG PILLOW

The hedgehog pillow is about 17 3/8" (44 cm) tall and 13 6/8" (35 cm) wide.

● ○ ○

WHAT YOU'LL NEED

- black topstitch thread
- polyfill stuffing
- wooden skewer (for turning)
- cardstock
- lightweight woven fusible interfacing:
  10" x 5 1/2" (26 x 14 cm)
- cotton fabric or velvet for the body:
  2 pieces of 17" x 20" (44 x 51 cm)
- cotton fabric for the paws:
  2 pieces of 2 7/8" x 3 1/4" (7.5 x 8.5 cm)
  2 pieces of 2 7/8" x 2 3/4" (7.5 x 6.5 cm)
- pile or cotton for the hedgehog snout:
  10" x 5 1/2" (26 x 14 cm)

PREPARING AND CUTTING THE MATERIAL

Read through the instructions before starting. Seam allowances are included in all pattern pieces where applicable.

1. Trace two **paws** (**4a**) onto the wrong side of two fabric rectangles of 2 7/8" x 3 1/4" (7.5 x 8.5 cm). Draw the lines CD and EF indicated on the pattern piece. Do not cut out yet. Prepare two identical rectangles of 2 7/8" x 2 3/4" (7.5 x 6.5 cm) for the back side of the paws.

2. Prepare a rectangle of 10" x 5 1/2" (24 x 14 cm) of fusible interfacing and a rectangle with the same dimensions in pile or cotton, for the snout.

3. Trace and cut the **body shape** (**4b**) onto a piece of cardstock.

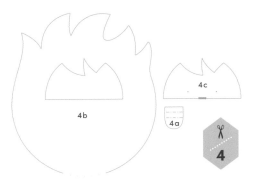

4. Fold the fabric between the two lines as shown in the pictures. Secure the material in place with a couple of pins. Do this for both paws.

5. Pin the folded pieces each on a piece of 2 7/8" x 2 3/4" (7.5 x 6.5 cm), right sides together, following the stitch line.

6. Sew along the line. Leave the side AB – as indicated on the pattern piece – open.

7. Remove the pins and cut the paws, using a seam allowance of 1/8" (3 mm) around, but don't leave a seam allowance on the open side.

8. Turn the paws right side out and stuff them right up to the CD line. Sew the opening close to the raw edge.

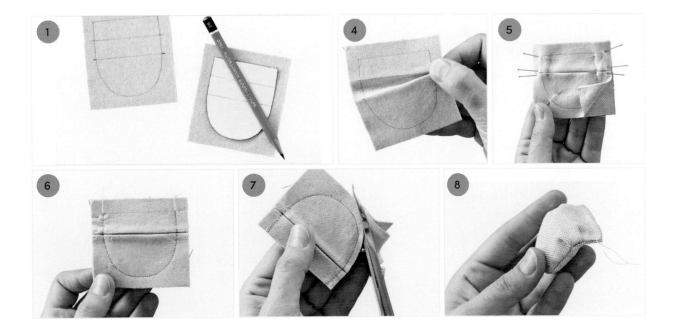

9. Take one rectangle of fabric for the front of the body. Put it with the right side facing up. Put the fusible interfacing on top where the snout will be, the adhesive side facing up. Use a white, beige or black fusible interfacing according to the color of the fabric.

10. Pin the fabric and the interfacing together. Center the body shape on the fabric and trace the perimeter of the **snout** (**4c**) on the interfacing. If you're using a geometric fabric, make sure you align the base of the snout with the fabric motifs.

11. Sew along the line of the snout. Cut out the center of the snout at 1/4" (6 mm) from the seam.

12. Cut the tips and the fabric in the corners along the seam allowance.

13. Turn the fusible interfacing through the opening to the wrong side of the fabric: the adhesive side of the interfacing touches the wrong side of the fabric now. Use a wooden skewer to gently push the spines out. Pin the interfacing in place.

14. Fix the interfacing to the fabric with the iron and remove the pins one by one as you progress. This will make the edge of the snout very well defined.

15. Put the body shape (**4b**) on top of the fabric, on the wrong side. Match the design of the snout with the opening and trace the edges of the body shape onto the fabric.

16. Cover the opening with a rectangle of cotton or pile with the right side facing down. Pin the fabric layers together. Turn the fabric right side up and topstitch the snout along the folded edge but leave the GH side – indicated on the pattern piece – open.

17. Insert the paws in the base of the snout, until the CD line is level with the folded edge, one on the right and one on the left. The folded side of the paws is facing the snout.

18. Pin and topstitch the GH line along the folded edge, locking the paws inside.

19. Pull the paws down. Sew them by hand from the wrong side of the fabric, in the middle of the paw, to fix them in this position. Cut off the excess seam allowance around the snout.

20. Embroider the eyes and the nose with a black topstitch thread and fix the loose ends on the wrong side of the fabric.

BODY

21. Put the front part of the pillow you've just made on top of the rectangle of fabric for the back part of the pillow, right sides together, align the edges and pin them together.

22. Carefully sew along the line of the hedgehog's body. Leave an opening at the base big enough to insert a hand.

23. Cut the hedgehog pillow using a seam allowance of 1/4" (6 mm) and a seam allowance of about 3/8" (10 mm) on the open side. Cut the tips and the fabric in the corners. Be very careful not to cut the seam.

24. Fold the edges of the opening as shown in the picture. To fold them, use a piece of cardstock with the round shape of the body. Fold the seam allowance over the cardstock and press it with the iron. Do one side and then the other.

25. Turn the pillow right side out. Use a wooden skewer to gently push the spines out.

26. Stuff the pillow with small amounts of polyfill stuffing at a time. Stuff the spines first, and then the body.

27. Sew the opening by hand.

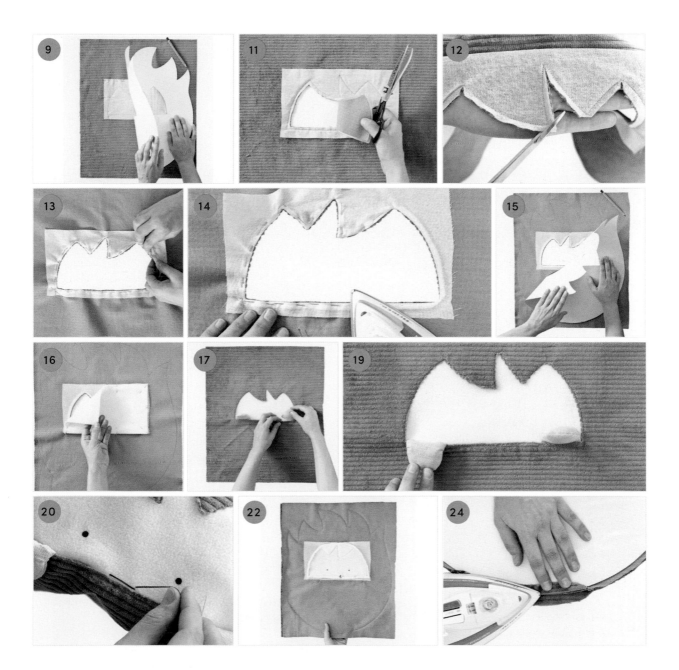

DRUM POUF FOR LITTLE ONES

*The pouf measures 14 5/8" (37 cm) in diameter
and 6 6/8" (17 cm) in height.*

● ● ○

- -

WHAT YOU'LL NEED

- topstitch thread
- paper clamps, Wonder Clips or little clothespins
- faux leather or strong cotton fabric:
  - 46" x 4 7/8" (116.8 x 12.2 cm) for the central band
  - 2 pieces of 46" x 1 1/2" (116.8 x 3.9 cm) for the side bands
  - 2 pieces of 46" x 7/8" (116.8 x 2.1 cm) for the piping bias tape (or buy ready-made piping with a seam allowance of 1/4" (6 mm))
  - 2 circles with a diameter of 14 7/8" (37.6 cm) for the top and bottom of the drum
- 1 1/2" (4 cm) thick foam:
  - 4 circles with a diameter of 14 7/8" (37.6 cm)
- hemp twine or piping cord for the piping bias

OPTIONAL

- polyfill fiber sheet (batting) of 46" x 4 1/4" (116.8 x 11 cm) (see step 5)

Note:

- -

It's important to choose a matching color for the thread, both for normal seams and topstitching. The material is stiffer then fabric, so the thread will always be visible in the seams.

- -

CUTTING AND PREPARING THE MATERIAL

Read through the instructions before starting. Seam allowances are included in all pattern pieces where applicable.

1. You can play with a fabric or leather combination of your preference for the side band of the drum. Cut a rectangle of 46" x 4 7/8" (116.8 x 12.2 cm) if you want to use a single piece of faux leather or fabric. The seam allowance of 1/4" (6 mm) is already included. Alternatively, trace 18 **rectangles (5a)** or 20 **triangles (5b)** on the wrong side of your chosen material to obtain a different design. Cut out all the pieces with a seam allowance of 1/4" (6 mm), as shown by the dotted line on the pattern piece. Once you have sewn the rectangles or the triangles together, you will have a band of the right dimensions.

   In this tutorial I used 18 rectangles of faux leather in three different colors: cream, light brown and pink. Find an example with triangles on page 43.

2. Cut two faux leather or fabric pieces of 46" x 1 1/2" (116.8 x 3.9 cm) for the side band trims. The seam allowance of 1/4" (6 mm) is already included.

3. Cut two faux leather or fabric strips of 46" x 7/8" (116.8 x 2.1 cm) to do the piping bias. Skip this step if you prefer to use ready-made piping.

4. Trace two **circles** (**5c**) on the wrong side of the faux leather or fabric for the top and bottom of your pouf. Trace the reference marks along the perimeter. Cut out with a 1/4" (6 mm) seam allowance, as shown by the dotted line on the pattern piece.

5. Trace four **shapes** (**5d**) on a 1 1/2" (4 cm) thick foam piece. The foam is a little bit bigger than the inside of the drum, so that the pouf will be taut. Cut the disks as precisely as possible along the line, holding the blade at 90°. The foam could also be cut easily with an (electrical) bread knife or a cutter. A scroll saw works great as well to cut this material. If the cut is not smooth, it can be visible on the outer surface of the drum. To solve this problem, you can cut the foam disks slightly smaller and insert a polyfill fiber sheet within the perimeter of the pouf (take a look at picture 22).

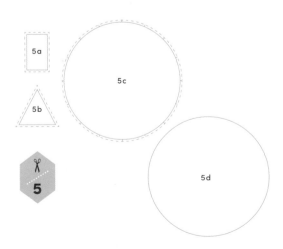

CENTRAL BAND

6. Put the rectangles (**5a**) two by two on top of each other, right sides together. Clamp and sew them at 1/4" (6 mm) from the edge, as shown in the picture.

7. Topstitch each side of the seam, pressing the seam allowances open. To sew the leather, use a long stitch length and, if necessary, a mount to keep the presser foot flat. A doubled leather cut-out works perfectly, as shown in the picture.

8. To finish the main band, fold it in half, right sides together, and clamp and sew the short sides. Press the seam allowances open and top-stitch close to the seam.

SIDE BANDS

9. Close the side band trims as described in step 8.

10. Put one side band on top of the main band, right sides together. Align the edges and match the seam of the side band with a seam between two rectangles. Clamp and sew at 1/4" (6 mm) from the edge. Remove the clamps as you stitch.

11. Unfold the side band and topstitch it close to the seam, catching the seam allowances on the wrong side of the fabric. Clamp and sew the other side band to the main band in the same way.

PIPING BIAS

If you use ready-made piping, make sure its seam allowance is 1/4" (6 mm) or trim it to this size. Align the raw edge of the piping to the free edge of the side bands, on the right side of the faux leather or fabric. Sew by machine with a suitable presser foot. Skip step 12-16 and go straight to step 17.

12. Fold the strips you've prepared for the piping bias in half, right sides together. Clamp and sew the short side at 1/4" (6 mm) from the edge. Cut the seam allowances at 1/8" (3 mm).

13. Put one strip on top of one side band, right sides together. Align the edges and match the seam with the seam of the side band. Clamp and sew at 1/8" (3 mm) from the edge. Remove the clamps as you proceed with the seam.

14. Take 47" (120 cm) of hemp twine and clamp one of the free ends to the edge you've just sewn.

Fold the little strip of faux leather or fabric in half and insert the twine inside. Clamp the first piece in place and start sewing by machine at 1/4" (6 mm) from the raw edge.

15. Stop the machine at about 1 1/2" (4 cm) from the end of the perimeter, cut the surplus hemp twine and secure the ends with a drop of glue. Continue sewing until you reach the end.

16. Repeat steps 13 to 15 for the piping bias on the other side band.

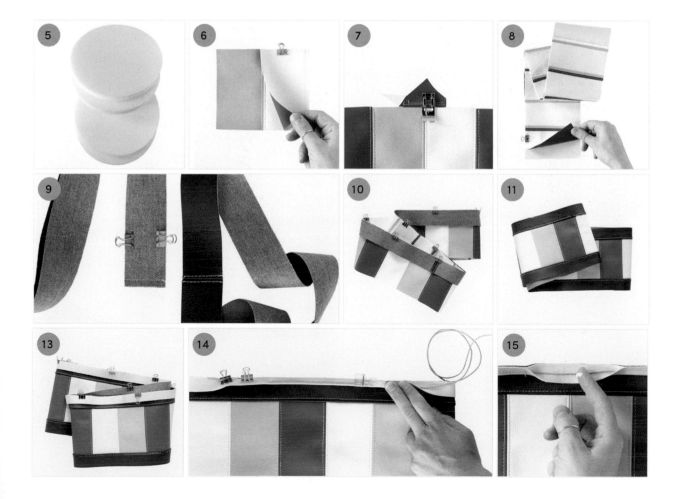

COMPLETE THE DRUM

17. Draw marks on the wrong side of the entire perimeter of the side bands at 2 7/8" (7.2 cm) from each other.

18. Clamp the top circle of the drum at one open edge of the faux leather or fabric tube, right sides together. Match each mark on the top circle with a mark on the side band, as shown in the picture.

19. Sew by machine around the circle at 1/4" (6 mm) from the edge.

20. Turn the drum right side out and insert a foam disk inside to verify that it fits perfectly. The foam disk has to be a bit bigger than the drum. If it is too big, trim the sides. If it is too small, make sure to insert the optional polyfill fiber sheet as shown at the step 22. Remove the disk and turn the drum wrong side out again.

21. Clamp the bottom circle at the open edge of the drum, right sides together. Match each mark on the bottom circle with a mark on the side band, as shown in the picture. Sew by machine a little more than halfway around the circle, at 1/4" (6 mm) from the edge.

22. Now you can leave the sides of the drum as they are or cover the edges of the foam disks with the optional polyfill fiber sheet, as mentioned in step 5. Glue the long edges of the sheet to the side bands of the drum or sew them by hand to the seam allowances.

23. Sew the short edges of the sheet together by hand.

24. Turn the drum right side out and insert a foam disk inside. Fold the disk in half to insert it and unfold it once inside.

25/26.
Push the foam disk down and inside against the seam allowances of the top circle. Check on the right side to see if the disk fits perfectly with the top of the drum.

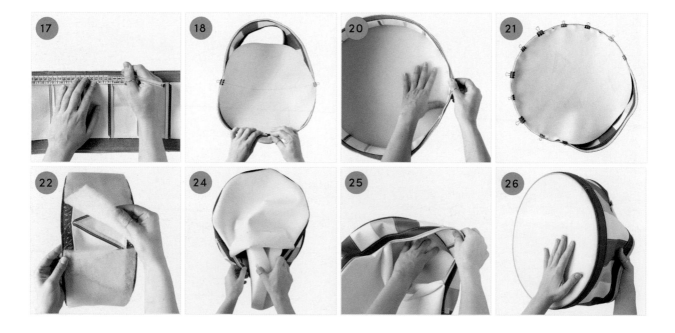

27. Insert the second foam disk inside the drum in the same way. Check with your fingers to see if the sides of the disks are aligned. If they aren't, you can see a line on the outside of the fabric. Do the same with the third disk.

28/29.
The fourth disk is the most difficult to insert. To slide it inside the drum, use a slippery fabric, like a silk scarf, or a plastic bag, as shown in the picture.

30. Remove the scarf or plastic bag and check if the disk is placed correctly inside the drum by inserting one hand above and your other hand below the last disk.

31. When you are satisfied with the fit of the foam disks inside the drum, match the marks on the wrong sides of the faux leather or fabric pieces and clamp the edges together.

32/33/34/35.
Sew the opening by hand. Draw the seam line onto the circle piece with a pencil. Thread a needle with a topstitch thread, make a knot at one end and fix it on the wrong side of the drum, exactly where the machine seam ends. Alternate one stitch along the seam line marked on the circle and one stitch on the piping bias, as shown in the pictures, to make the two edges join exactly.

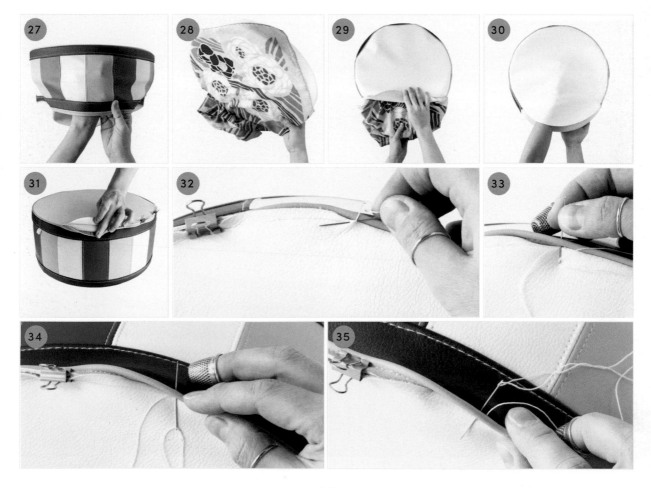

"My handmade world is concocted in my laboratory, which is actually a fancy term for my living room: a rather small and not very light place, so it needs some preparation before I can start sewing. I move the "work area", aka the table to the window. My tools and materials are lined up like little soldiers ready to fight. I put on some music and start to work while humming softly. When I take a tea break and look around the room, I realize I have turned the place completely upside down and I find my 'soldiers' everywhere, caught in the creative chaos. Order is just a starting point, and then the ideas and creative energy explode."

POLAR BEAR – PAPERWEIGHT, PEN HOLDER

The polar bear is 3 3/8" (8.5 cm) tall.

• • •

- -

WHAT YOU'LL NEED

- glue
- large embroidery needle with a pointed end
- masking tape or transparent adhesive tape
- topstitch extra strong thread
- cardstock
- cling film
- thin sand
- faux leather, possibly matt, soft to the touch and non-stretchable:
    10 5/8" x 8 5/8" (27 x 22 cm)
- 3 mm thick felt:
    33/8" x 3 3/8" (8.5 x 8.5 cm)

Note:

It's important to choose a matching color for the thread, both for normal seams and topstitching. The material is stiffer then fabric, so the thread will always be visible in the seams.

CUTTING AND PREPARING THE MATERIAL

Read through the instructions before starting. Seam allowances are included in all pattern pieces where applicable.

1. If you have a steady hand, trace the pattern pieces to carbon paper. Alternatively, you can photocopy the pieces. There are a lot of exact points to transfer onto the faux leather, which makes it hard to trace it by hand. Glue the copied pieces on a piece of cardstock and carefully cut out all the pieces of cardstock along the cutting line. These will now be used to trace each bear shape on the faux leather. Place the **body** (**6a**), the **pen holder** (**6b**), the **pen holder base** (**6c**), two **ears** (**6d**) and the **base** (**6e**) on the right side of the faux leather as shown in the picture. Temporarily fix the cardstock onto the pieces of faux leather with some paper tape (check first to see if the tape does not damage the material).

2. Take a large embroidery needle with a pointed end and transfer all the dots illustrated on the pattern piece onto the faux leather. Put a piece of cardstock or other suitable material under the faux leather to avoid damaging the table top and the needle tip. The transferred points on the faux leather will help you to make perfect seams.

3. Trace the outline of all parts of the bear on the faux leather with a pen.

4. Remove the cardstock shapes and cut out each piece drawn on the faux leather exactly along the inside of the traced outline, as shown in the picture. In this way, completely removing the pen mark, you will get shapes identical to the pattern pieces.

5. Cut the pen holder hole in the same way.

6. Trace the **base reinforcement** (**6h**) on the felt. Trace the **base reinforcement** (**6h**) and the **pen holder reinforcements** (**6f**) and (**6g**) on a piece of cardstock. Cut out all the pieces along the marked line.

7. Glue the cardstock base reinforcement to the felt and leave it to dry. Glue the pen holder base (**6c**) to the pen holder reinforcement (**6g**) and leave it to dry.

8. Position the pen holder (**6b**) next to the hole on the bear body, wrong sides together. Align the first point impressed in the pen holder piece with the point at the bottom center of the hole. Pass 28" (70 cm) of topstitch thread through these two points. Divide the thread evenly on both sides of the points and thread each end in a needle.

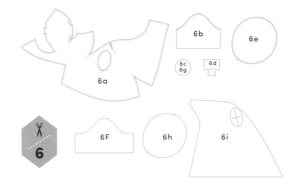

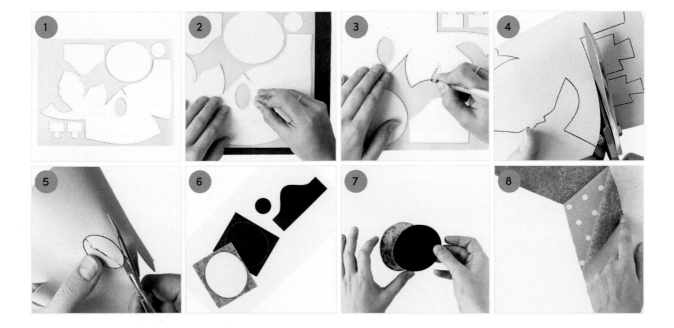

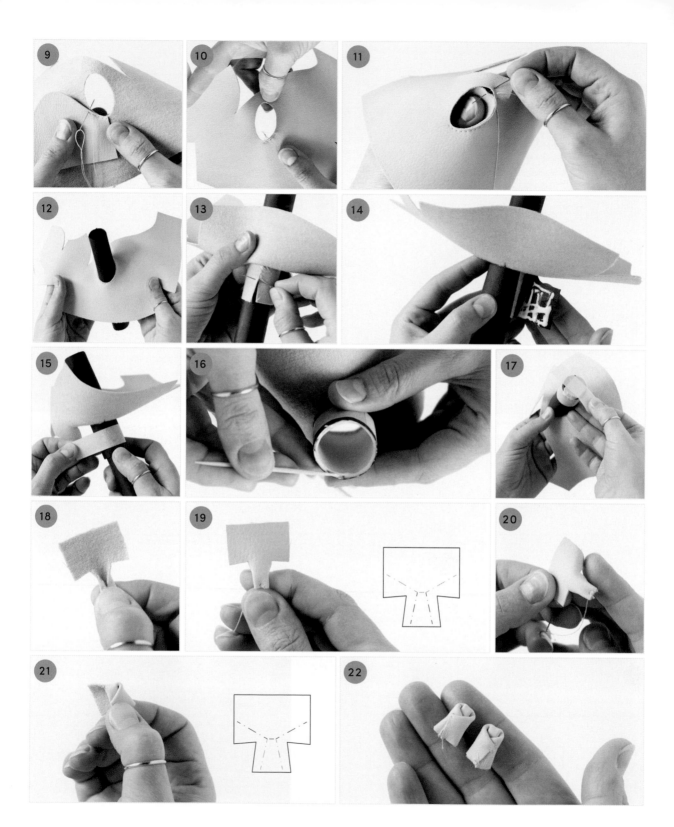

9/10/11.

Create the seam hole by hole by alternating the use of needles as shown in the pictures. Follow the points impressed on the faux leather to obtain a perfect topstitch on both sides of the work. Carefully sew the perimeter of the hole by hand. When you reach the starting point, fix the threads at the wrong side of the pieces of faux leather and **cut only one of them**.

12. Insert a cylinder with a circumference of 3 1/8" (8 cm) inside the hole. If you have nothing of this dimension, roll up a piece of cardstock.

13. With the thread remaining of steps 9/10/11 sew the edges of the pen holder as shown in the picture.

14. Spread the pen holder reinforcement (**6f**) with glue and paste it around the pen holder in the faux leather.

15. Fasten it with a piece of transparent adhesive tape. Leave it to dry before you advance to the next step.

16. Glue the reinforcement (**6g**) to the wrong side of the pen holder base. Remove the cylinder from the hole and paste the pen holder base on the bottom of the tube, putting a bit of glue along the perimeter of the hole. The right side of the base is on the inside.

17. Secure it with a piece of transparent adhesive tape.

18/19.

Fold the ear along the red lines, on the wrong side of the faux leather, as shown in the figure and in the pictures, and sew the two edges on the bottom side by hand.

20/21.

Fold the ear once again along the red line and over the part folded in step 18/19, as shown in the figure and in the pictures. Fold the sides one after another.

22. Lock the edges into place with a couple of hand stitches. Repeat steps 18 to 22 for the second ear.

23. Fold the bear's head as indicated in the figure, right sides together. Sew the edges marked with red and blue dots, starting from the nose. Pass 22" (55 cm) of topstitch thread through the first two points impressed in the faux leather, as shown in the figure and in the picture. Divide the thread evenly on both sides of the points and thread each end of the thread in a needle.

24/25.

Carry on the seam little by little by alternating the use of needles. Follow the points impressed on the faux leather to obtain a perfect topstitch.

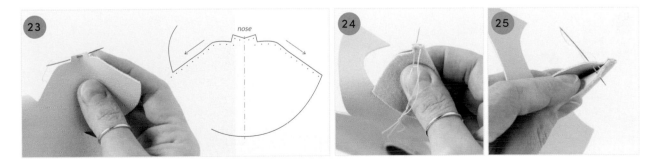

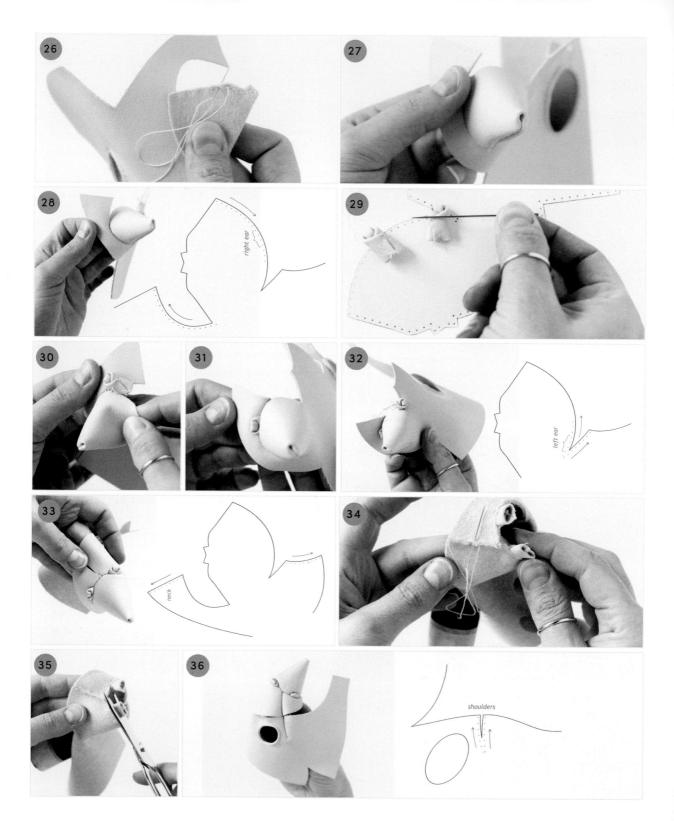

26. Carefully sew the side of the head by hand. When you reach the final points, tie the threads **without** cutting them.

27. Turn the head right side out, leaving the nose inwards.

28. With the threads remaining, continue sewing the head to the body along the sides highlighted with red and blue points in the figure and the picture. Always keep the faux leather right sides together.

29/30.
Include the right ear in the seam, at the height shown in the picture. Fix the ear to the four points that are highlighted. Look at picture 31 to see the result.

31. When you reach the middle point of the head, tie the threads and cut the loose ends.

32. Cut 18" (45 cm) of thread and sew the other side of the head in the same way, as shown in the figure and in the picture, including the left ear in the seam. When you reach the middle point of the head, tie the threads without cutting them.

33/34.
Sew the bear's neck, right sides together, with the threads that remained from the previous step. Tie the threads and cut the loose ends.

35. Cut off the excess of the ears as shown in the picture.

BODY

36. With 12" (30 cm) of thread and two needles, sew the crease on the bear's shoulders as shown in the picture, right sides together. The figure indicates which edges we're referring to. Tie the threads and cut the loose ends. This two-needle technique will make your seam solid and steady.

37/38.
Sew the edges together as shown in the image, from the left side of the shoulders to the front of the bear, as illustrated by the red and blue points in the figure. Cut 22" (55 cm) of thread and sew the faux leather, again with two needles, right sides together.

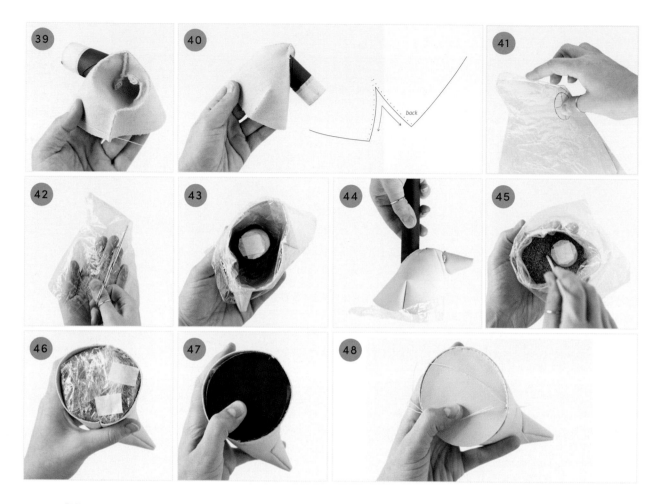

39. When you reach the point on the bear's front, tie the threads and cut the loose ends.

40. Sew the crease on the bear's back with 14" (35 cm) of thread and two needles, right sides together, as shown in the picture and the figure. Tie the threads and cut the loose ends.

41. In this step, we'll make a plastic bag to fill the pen holder with sand. Put two layers of cling film with the dimensions of an A4 sheet onto each other. Wrap the **cardstock template (6i)** in the cling film. Leave a margin of 4/8" (1 cm) of cling film at the top of the cardstock and fold it to close the bag, as shown in the figure. Draw a cross over the pen holder hole indicated on the pattern piece.

42. Remove the cardstock, put a hand inside the bag and cut the film along the cross marks.

43. Carefully put the bag inside the bear and pass the pen holder cylinder through the hole made in the cling film. Push the film against the inner sides of the body, using a pen.

44. To avoid the risk of crushing the penholder, insert the cardstock cylinder again.

45. Pour the sand into the bag, little by little, making sure everything is firmly filled. Repeatedly pierce the sand with a small stick to fill any empty spaces. Fill the bear almost to the top, the sand should be pressed together.

46. Cut out the cling film 2" (5 cm) from the base of the bear. Bend the edges to close the bag, but don't pull them. Hold the film into place with a piece of transparent adhesive tape.

47. Put the base of felt and cardstock over the cling film, matching the marks with the back and front of the bear.

48. Cut 28" (70 cm) of thread and sew the base of faux leather to the body of the bear, wrong sides together. Use the two-needle technique, starting from the back. Once you have sewn along the perimeter, you can fix and cut the threads.

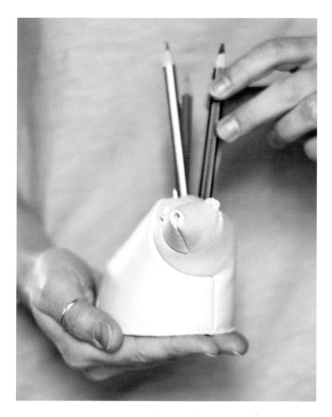

RABBIT PILLOW

The rabbit pillow is about 15" (38 cm) tall, plus 7" (18 cm) for the ears and 12 5/8" (32 cm) wide.

●○○

- -

WHAT YOU'LL NEED

- brown and black topstitch thread
- polyfill stuffing
- cardstock
- firm canvas cotton fabric for the body:
  2 pieces of 16" x 12" (40 x 30 cm)
- pile or cotton for the rabbit head and tail:
  17 1/2" x 21" (43.5 x 53 cm)
- cotton fabric for the right ear:
  4" x 8" (10 x 20 cm)
- cotton fabric for the nose:
  5 2/8" x 2 7/8" (13 x 7 cm)

PREPARING AND CUTTING THE MATERIAL

Read through the instructions before starting. Seam allowances are included in all pattern pieces where applicable.

1. Trace two patterns of **head (7a)** onto the wrong side of the pile fabric, one with and one without the right ear, as shown in the picture. Trace the **tail (7b)** as well. Cut out the pieces of the head and tail with a 1/4" (6 mm) seam allowance, as shown by the dotted line on the pattern piece.

2. Trace two patterns of **body (7c)** onto the wrong side of two rectangles of fabric of 16" x 12" (40 x 30 cm). Cut out the pieces with a 1/4" (6 mm) seam allowance, as shown by the dotted line on the pattern piece.

3. Trace the **right ear (7d)** and the **nose (7e)** onto the wrong side of two different fabrics. Cut out the pieces with a 1/4" (6 mm) seam allowance, as shown by the dotted line on the pattern piece.

4. Trace and cut the **nose shape (7f)** and the **triangle shape (7g)** onto a piece of cardstock.

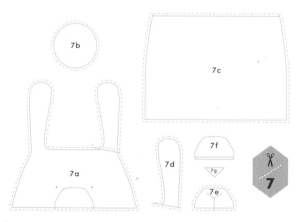

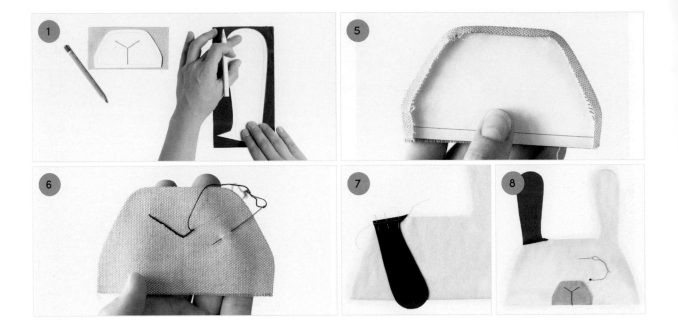

NOSE

5. Fold the upper and side edges of the nose over the shape (**7f**), as shown in the picture. Put the cardstock on the wrong side of the fabric, matching the design of the nose, and iron the edges.

6. Draw the lines of the nose on the right side of the fabric and embroider them with a brown topstitch thread. Secure the loose end on the wrong side of the fabric.

HEAD

7. Put the right ear to the piece of the head without it, right sides together. Pin and sew along the AB line. Remove the pins and press the seam with your fingers.

8. Put the nose on top of the head and pin it in place. Topstitch close to the folded edge of the nose. Embroider the eyes with a black topstitch thread. Secure the loose end on the wrong side of the fabric.

9. Put the front side on top of the back side of the head, right sides together. Pin them and sew around, at 1/4" (6 mm) from the edge. Don't close the base side.

10. Clip the seam allowances along the curved edges. Be careful not to cut the seams.

11. Turn the head right side out and stuff the ears. Use a wooden skewer or a pencil to push polyfill stuffing inside. Fill them until you get the desired effect.

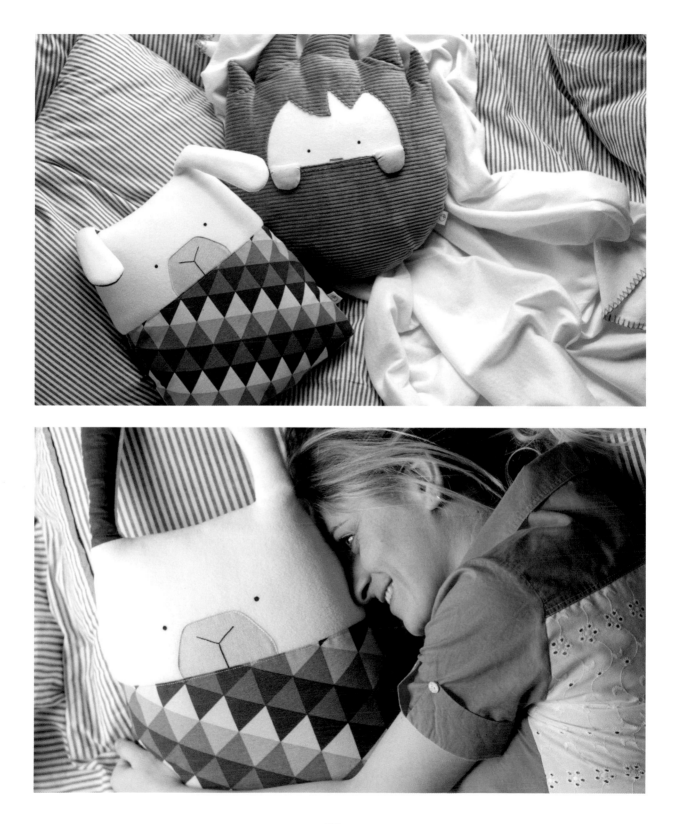

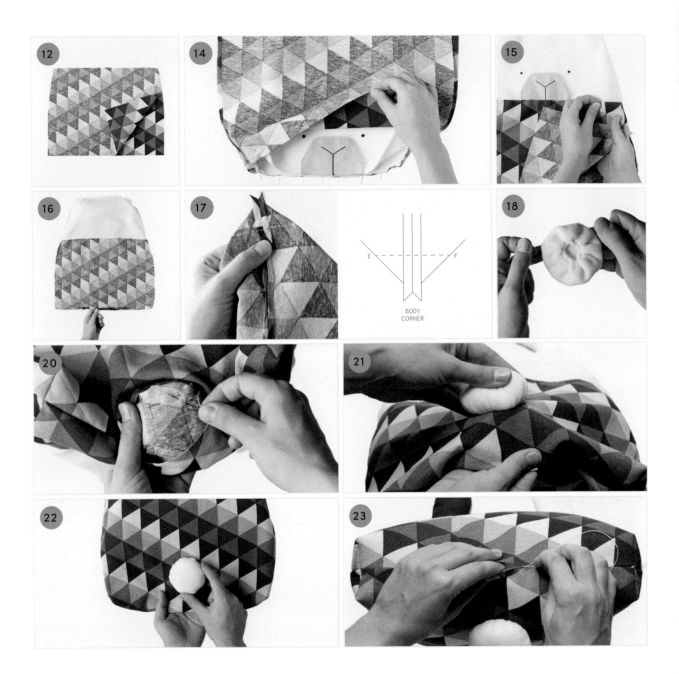

BODY
CORNER

BODY

12. Put the two body pieces (**7c**) of fabric on top of each other, right sides together. Pin them and sew along the two perimeter sections indicated by the letters CD.

13. Press the seam allowances open.

14. Insert the head between the two fabric pieces of the body, right sides together, as shown in the picture. The seams on the sides of the body should match the seams on the sides of the head. Pin the base edge of the head and the upper edge of the body together and sew along the edge with a 1/4" (6 mm) seam allowance.

15. Turn the rabbit right side out. Fold and pin the seam allowance between the head and the body downward. Topstitch the body along and close to the edge.

16. Turn the rabbit wrong side out again. Pin the open edges of the body together and sew them at 1/4" (6 mm) from the edge. Leave an opening at the base of the pillow big enough to insert your hand. Fold and iron the edges at the opening, as shown in the picture. Do one side first, and then the other.

17. Fold the corners at the base of the pillow, as shown in the picture. Match the seams on the side and the base of the body. Open the seam allowances and pin it all in place. Use the triangle shape (**7g**), drawn in the pattern, to mark the EF line on the fabric and sew along this line. Turn the pillow right side out.

TAIL

18. Do a running stitch* around the tail or sew around by machine on the longest stitch length, setting the thread tension at the minimum, without securing the thread at the beginning and at the end. Pull the running stitch to make the fabric curl and make sure the right side of the fabric is on the outside. Tie the threads and cut the ends.

19. Stuff the tail with a bit of polyfill stuffing.

20/21. Put the tail on the back of the pillow, with the hole toward the contact point, at 3 1/2" (9 cm) from the bottom edge. Reach through the opening on the base of the rabbit to sew the tail to the body by hand. Stitch all around the hole of the tail.

22. Stuff the pillow with small amounts of polyfill stuffing at a time, leaving no gaps.

23. Sew the opening by hand using a ladder stitch*.

* see p. 10

PLAYFUL CAT – KEYCHAIN, PINCUSHION, PENDANT, LUCKY CHARM

The cat is 3 1/2" (9 cm) long, 2 1/2" (6 cm) tall and 2" (5 cm) wide.

● ● ○

- -

WHAT YOU'LL NEED

- polyfill stuffing
- wooden skewer (for turning)
- waxed cord 5" (13 cm)
- brown nylon thread ø .008" (0.20 mm)
- 2 small black beads
- plain and/or printed cotton fabric:
    8" x 9 1/2" (20 x 24 cm) for the body, head
    and back head
    6" x 6" (15 x 15 cm) for the belly and the ears

OPTIONAL

- metal keyring
- woven fusible interfacing (as reinforcement if the fabric of your choice is very thin)

PREPARING AND CUTTING THE FABRIC

Read through the instructions before starting. Seam allowances are included in all pattern pieces where applicable.

1. Place and trace the pattern pieces onto the wrong side of the larger piece of fabric and cut out one piece of the **head** (**8a**), two mirrored pieces of the **body** (**8b**) and three pieces of the **back head** (**8e**) with a seam allowance of 1/4" (6 mm). Mark the location of the eyes, the nose and the whiskers with chalk or a fabric pen.

2. Trace one piece of the **belly** (**8c**) on the wrong side of the other fabric and cut out with a seam allowance of 1/4" (6 mm) as shown by the dotted line on the pattern piece. Also trace two pieces of the **ear** (**8d**) and cut out without seam allowance.

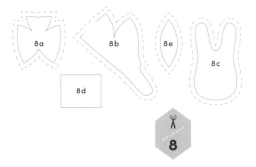

3. Cut 11 3/4" (30 cm) of colored thin cotton thread, matching the color of the cat. Double or triple the thread to obtain the right thickness for the tail. Fold the thread in half around a pin, as shown in the figure.

4. Twist the two tresses in the same direction with the tips of your fingers. Twist them one by one, keeping hold of the ends so that they don't unwind. Twist them very close while not loosening the tension on the threads. Then take away the pin, and let them roll up around each other.

5. Tie a knot to close the tail at the length of 4" (10 cm) and cut the excess thread.

BODY

6. Take the body pieces (**8b**). Close the darts on both sides of the body, and make sure to sew a curved line which tapers to a point by carefully following the marked stitching line.

7. Pin the tail on the right side of one of the body pieces at the location of the dart lines.

8. Put the two parts of the body on top of each other, right sides together. Pin and sew them from point 1 to point 2 and from point 3 to point 4. This will leave an opening for turning the body in a later step.

9. Remove the pins and trim the curved seam allowance above the paws, as shown in the figure.

10. Pin the waxed cord, folded in half, on the right side of the belly (**8c**), at the center of one paw.

11. Put the body on top of the belly, right sides together. Pin or baste them and sew all around. Remove the pins or basting.

12. Make a knot at the end of the waxed cord and cut the seam allowances as shown in the figure.

13. Turn the cat body right side out. Use a wooden skewer to carefully push out the paws. Stuff it with polyfill stuffing and sew the opening by hand.

EARS

14. Take the two ear rectangles (**8d**). Fold a rectangle in half, right side out. Fold it twice as shown in the figure, to make the left ear of the cat. Sew as shown and cut the excess seam allowance. Do the same with the other rectangle to make the right ear, but fold in the opposite direction so that the ears will look similar and mirror each other.

HEAD

15. Take the head (**8a**) and the three back head pieces (**8e**).

16. Close all the darts on the head as shown in the figure: pin the seam allowance right sides together at each slit, and sew from the point to the raw edge.

17. Turn the head right side out and pin the ears as shown in the figure. Align the center of the ears with the dart lines on top of the head. Fold the seam allowances of the darts outwards.

18. Sew two back head parts (**8e**), right sides together, as shown in the figure, leaving an opening at the middle of the seam for turning the head in a later step. Sew the third piece to one of the free sides of the two back head pieces you've just attached.

19. Put the back head on top of the front head, right sides together. Pin or baste them together and sew all around. Remove the pins or basting.

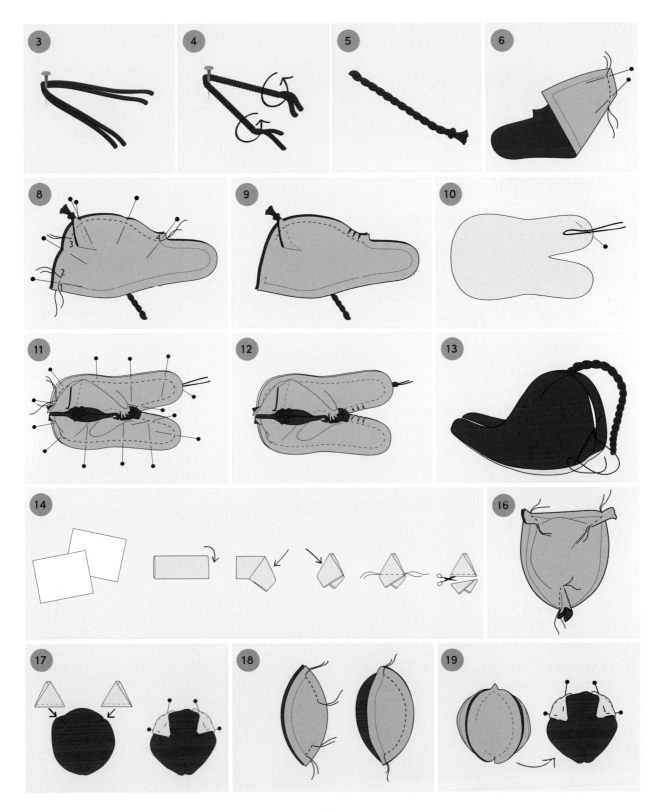

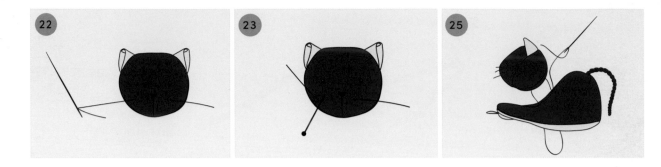

20. Turn the head right side out through the opening left on the back side. Stuff the head with polyfill stuffing while keeping the ears folded forward. The opening will be sewn closed in a later step.

21. Embroider the nose with black thread. Hide the knots inside the head. Fix the two small beads at eye level by passing the thread through the head.

22. Make the cat's whiskers with brown nylon, three whiskers on each side. Thread a needle with nylon and make a knot at 1 1/2" (4 cm) from the free end. Pass the needle inside the cat's face, going in and out at both sides of the nose. Gently pull the thread so that the knot will not touch the cat's snout.

23. Remove the needle and make a second knot at the exit point of the thread. Use a needle tip to make the knot very near the cat's snout.

24. Do the same for the rest of the whiskers. Cut them to 5/8" (1.5 cm) in length. Sew the opening on the back side of the head by hand.

ALL THE PIECES TOGETHER

25. Sew the head to the body as shown in the figure. Pass the thread more than once to make a strong seam. Secure the thread and hide the excess thread inside the body.

If you want to use the cat as a keychain, you only have to add a metal ring to the waxed cord that was previously inserted into one of his paws.

JO HANDMADE DESIGN

" My grandmother and her sewing
machine always have been the most
important muses for my work, and I also
learned a lot from following my father
around like a puppy when he built this or
that inside or outside the house. My other
great passion is drawing, and I'm a big
fan of cartoons and comics. I really love
the animated films by the Japanese artist
Hayao Miyazaki, like Future Boy Conan,
which was the first one to steal my heart.
I closely guard my manga collection and
I'm a huge fan of the Peanuts and
Calvin and Hobbes.

HEDGEHOG DOORSTOP

The hedgehog is 9 5/8" (24.5 cm) tall.

●●●

- -

WHAT YOU NEED

- stitching awl or large embroidery needle with a pointed end
- wooden skewer (for turning)
- masking tape or transparent adhesive tape
- topstitch thread
- black cotton thread
- cardstock
- polyfill stuffing
- a plastic bag
- thin sand
- faux leather, possibly matt, soft to the touch and non-stretchable:
    24" x 14" (60 x 35 cm) for the body
- faux suede or strong cotton fabric:
    11" x 5 1/2" (28 x 14 cm) for the head
    2 pieces of 6 1/2" x 3 3/8" (16.5 x 8.5 cm) for the ears
- 1/8" (3 mm) thick felt:
    5 1/8" x 3 1/8" (13 x 8 cm)
- 3/4" (20 mm) polyfill fiber sheet:
    11" x 11" (28 x 28 cm)

OPTIONAL

- tweezers (to stuff the spines with the polyfill fiber sheet, see step 28)

Note

It's important to choose a matching color for the thread, both for normal seams and topstitching. The material is stiffer then fabric, so the thread will always be visible in the seams.

CUTTING AND PREPARING THE MATERIAL

Read through the instructions before starting. Seam allowances are included in all pattern pieces where applicable.

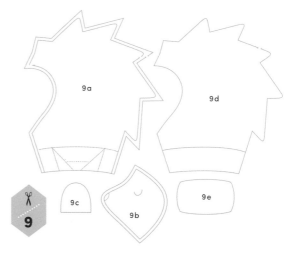

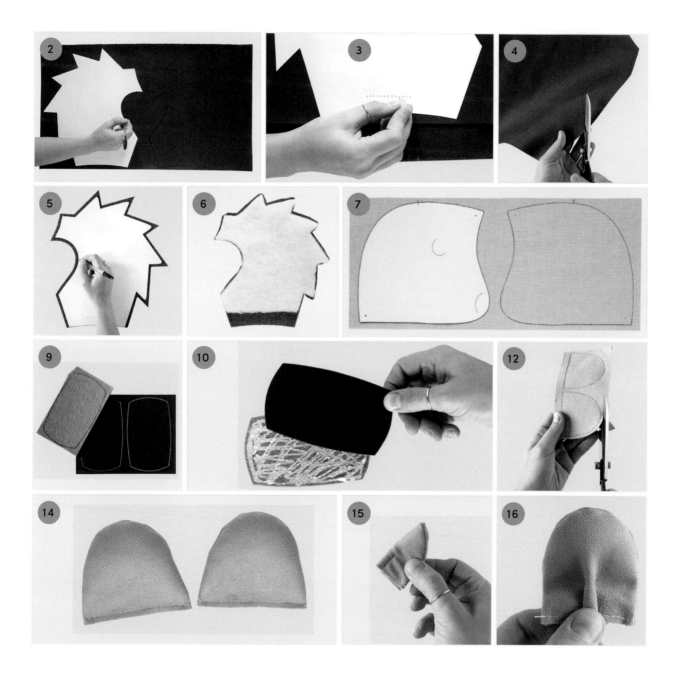

1. Trace or photocopy the patterns on a piece of cardstock, so it will be easier to draw each hedgehog shape on the faux leather and fabric. Carefully cut out all the pieces of cardstock along the perimeter.

2. Trace two mirrored patterns of the **body (9a)** on the right side of the faux leather with a pen. Insert the paper tape between the cardstock and the pieces of faux leather to fix them together (check first to see if the tape does not damage the material).

3. Take a stitching awl or a large embroidery needle with a pointed end and transfer the dots illustrated in the pattern on the faux leather. Put a piece of cardstock or other suitable material under the faux leather to avoid damaging the table top and the needle tip. The transferred points on the faux leather will guide you in making the last hand stitching.

4. Remove the piece of cardstock and cut out the pieces drawn on the faux leather exactly along the inside of the traced outline. In this way, completely removing the pen mark, you will get shapes identical to the pattern pieces.

5. Use the **body shape (9d)** to mark the lines (to sew by machine later) on the wrong side of the body pieces.

6. Cut out the same **body shape (9d)** from a 20 mm polyfill fiber sheet. The bottom edge should be cut along the AB line as shown in the pattern.

7. Trace two mirrored patterns of the **head (9b)** onto the wrong side of the faux suede. Draw the reference mark for the ears and the two points C and D in the corners. Cut out the pieces with a 1/4" (6 mm) seam allowance, as shown by the green, continuous line on the pattern piece. Draw the eye and the perimeter of the nose with a crayon on the right side of the head pieces.

8. Prepare two pieces of faux suede with measurements of 6 1/2" x 3 3/8" (16.5 x 8.5 cm) for the ears.

9. Draw one **base reinforcement (9e)** on the felt and two identical pieces of cardstock. Cut them out along the marked line.

10. Glue the two pieces of cardstock together, and glue them to the felt base. Put the base reinforcement aside to dry.

EARS

11. Trace two patterns of the **ear (9c)** on the wrong side of a piece of faux suede.

12. Put the two rectangles of fabric on top of each other, right sides together. Sew the curved lines, but leave the edge at the base open. Cut out both ears **(9c)** with a 1/8" (3 mm) seam allowance, but cut the base edge without seam allowance. Turn the ears right side out. Use your fingers to push the fabric through the opening.

13. Fill only the top half of the ears with polyfill stuffing.

14. Pin the bottom edges of the ears and sew them at 1/8" (3 mm) from the raw edge.

15. Fold the two ears in half and sew as shown in the picture. Make a seam of 3/4" (2 cm) long, 1/4" (6 mm) from the folded center.

16. Open the ears and press the small crease on the back with your fingers.

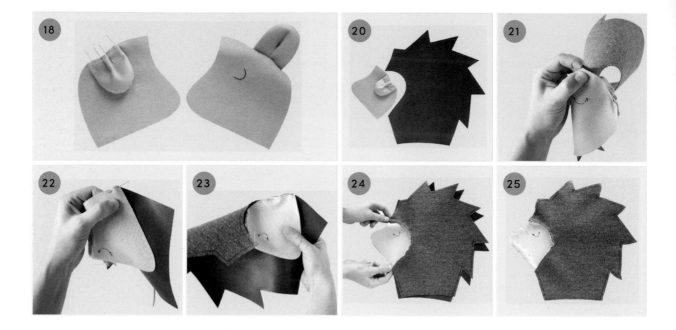

HEAD

17. Embroider the eyes with a black cotton thread using the stem stitch* or another stitch of your choice.

18. Pin the ears on the right side of the head pieces, as shown in the picture. Align the center of each ear with the mark on the head sides. Sew them together at 1/8" (3 mm) from the edge, so they will not move during the following steps.

PUT ALL THE PIECES TOGETHER

19. Clip the seam allowance of the two body pieces in the inward curve. The small cuts should only be 1/8" (3 mm) deep.

20/21/22.
Put the sides of the head on top of each corresponding side of the body, right sides together. Match points C and D and secure them with a pin, as shown in the pictures. Pin the material within the seam allowance, to make sure you don't damage the visible side of the faux leather.

23. Pin the rest of the seam allowances between the sides of the head and the body. Carefully sew them together, leaving a seam allowance of 1/4" (6 mm). Remove the pins as you proceed with the seam. Stiff faux leather – as in my case – instead of soft faux leather makes this step more difficult.

24. Put the two sides of the hedgehog on top of each other, as shown in the picture. Secure them together with a hand stitch exactly at points C and D, so the two layers of the hedgehog can't move at these two points during the following steps.

25. Pin along the entire perimeter of the hedgehog, as shown in the picture. Sew by machine along the line drawn on the wrong side of the body, removing the pins as you proceed with the seam. Sew the head with a 1/4" (6 mm) seam allowance.

26. Trim the seam allowances in the corners. Leave a seam allowance of 1/8" (3 mm) along the round tips of the spines and around the nose.

* see p. 10

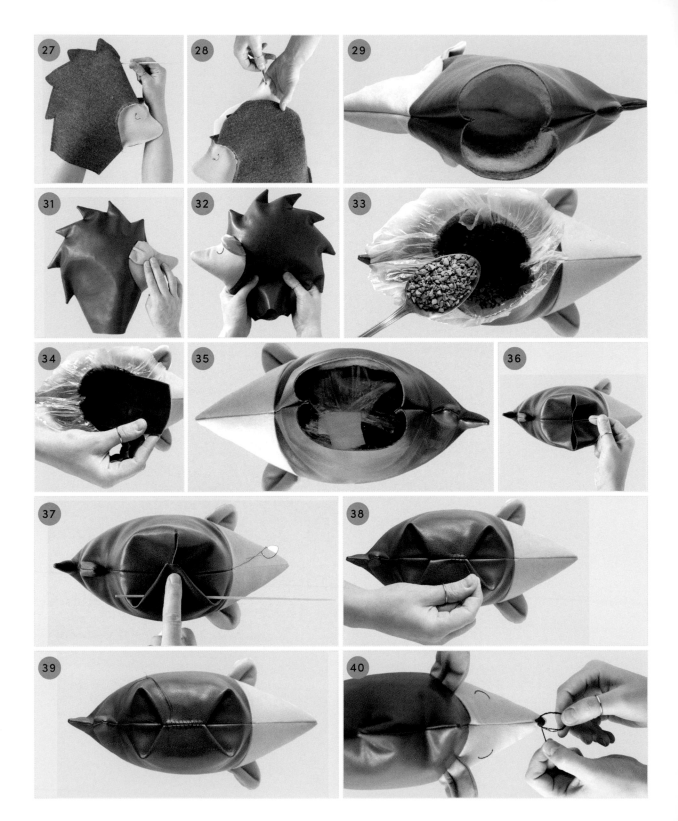

27. Gently push the hedgehog's spines inside the body with a wooden skewer.

28. Insert the spines of the polyfill shape into the corresponding faux leather spines, as shown in the picture. Use tweezers or a wooden skewer to push them until they reach the tips. Divide the polyfill sheet in two layers with your fingers, without separating the edges at the sides, creating a bag. This additional layer inside the hedgehog allows you to make a uniform surface on the outside of the doorstop and to hide the dividing line between soft polyfill stuffing and sand.

29. Gently turn the hedgehog right side out making sure you include the polyfill shape inside the hedgehog.

30. Stuff the hedgehog by pressing the polyfill stuffing inside. Start with pushing a bit of polyfill stuffing into the spines with the help of a wooden skewer.

31. Stuff the hedgehog while keeping the ears folded towards the head. By firmly stuffing the body with the ears fixed in this position, the polyfill stuffing will keep the seam allowance inside the head in the opposite direction, which will give the ears the right position in the end result.

32. Stuff a little more than half of the body, as shown in the picture.

33. Sit down and keep the hedgehog between your legs. Insert a plastic bag inside the bottom of the body and pour the sand into it, little by little. To fill every single empty space, repeatedly pierce the sand with a stick, being careful not to pierce the bag. Fill the hedgehog up to 2" (5 cm) from the open edge. The sand should be firmly pressed together.

Note

If your synthetic leather is as stiff as mine, you can use coarse sand, as you can see in the picture. If your synthetic leather is thin and soft, choose fine-grained sand to make sure the shape of the grains isn't visible through the hedgehog.

34. Put the base reinforcement (**9e**) on top of the sand, as shown in the picture. The felt side should be facing down.

35. Cut the plastic bag even with the edge of the faux leather at the bottom of the hedgehog. Bend the plastic over the base reinforcement to close the bag, but don't pull it. Secure the edges with a piece of transparent adhesive tape.

36. Fold the edges of the hedgehog's base as shown in the picture, and make sure the seams are touching each other. Hand stitch them in the middle with a long and strong thread, but **do not cut** the excess thread. You will still need it in step 38, to close the base.

37. Fold the faux leather once again in the other direction, forming a triangle, as shown in the picture.

38. Fold under 5/8" (1.5 cm) of the tip. Repeat steps 37 to 38 on the other side of the hedgehog's base. Use the remaining thread from step 36 to sew the folded sides at the hedgehog's base together. Start from the center and work towards one side following the dots impressed on the faux leather (see step 3).

39. At the end of the seam, go back towards the other side and then go back to the center. Tie the thread and cut the loose ends.

40. Turn and place the hedgehog on the desk. Use a black cotton thread to embroider the nose, as shown in the picture. Turn the thread around the nose in and out on both sides of the snout, following the traces drawn on the fabric. Start from the top of the nose and work to the bottom point, advancing just a few millimeters at a time to cover all the fabric underneath with the thread. Tie off the thread or work the ends in and cut the loose ends.

"*I remember a lot of funny episodes with hedgehogs, and they're all linked to my dog. My dog barks in a bizarre way whenever he finds a hedgehog, I even call it the 'hedgehog alarm'. Maybe he thinks that the hedgehog is an animated ball, but when he tries to play with one, the spines prick his muzzle, and then he'll vent his surprise by an uninterrupted barking at the poor, frightened hedgehog ball.*"

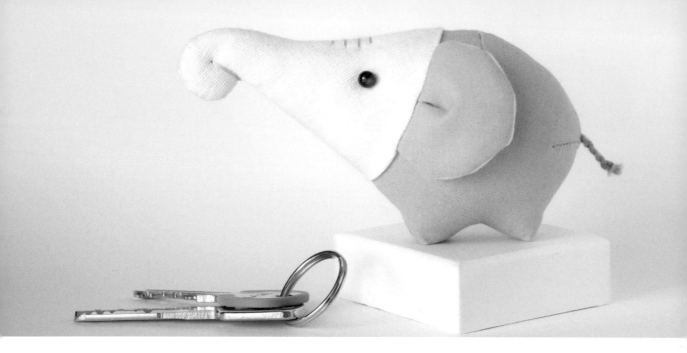

LINO THE ELEPHANT – KEYCHAIN, PINCUSHION, PENDANT, LUCKY CHARM

The elephant is 4 3/4" (12 cm) long, 2 3/8" (6 cm) tall and 1 5/8" (4 cm) wide.

● ● ○

- -

WHAT YOU'LL NEED

- polyfill stuffing
- wooden skewer (for turning)
- cardstock
- plain and/or printed woven cotton fabric:
    7 1/2" x 4 1/2" (19 x 12 cm) for the head
    2 pieces of 5" x 2 1/2" (13 x 7 cm) for the ears
        in 2 different fabrics
    8" x 5" (20 x 13 cm) for the body
- topstitch thread
- cotton thread
- nylon thread ø .008" (0.20 mm)
- 2 black beads ø 1/4" (6 mm)

OPTIONAL

- woven fusible interfacing (as reinforcement if the fabric of your choice is very thin, and for your head fabric for the keychain option)
- metal key ring (If you want to transform the elephant into a keychain, you can use a big needle to make a hole in the center of the trunk and insert a metal key ring when your elephant is ready. Make sure to interface the head fabric if you want to use the elephant as a keychain, and optionally use an anti-fray product on the raw edges of the hole.)

CUTTING AND PREPARING THE MATERIAL

Read through the instructions before starting. Seam allowances are included in all pattern pieces where applicable.

1. Trace two **ear** (**10a**) shapes onto the wrong side of one of your ear's fabrics. Put aside.

2. Trace two patterns of the **head** (**10b**) onto the wrong side of the fabric. Cut out the pieces with a 1/4" (6 mm) seam allowance, as shown by the dotted line on the pattern piece.

3. Draw the folding guide (**10c**) on a piece of cardstock. Cut out the piece.

4. Trace two patterns of **body** (**10d**) onto the wrong side of the fabric. Copy the reference mark for the ears. Cut out the pieces with a 1/4" (6 mm) seam allowance, as shown by the dotted line on the pattern piece.

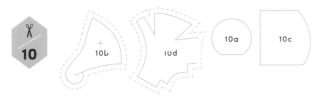

EARS

5. Put the fabric pieces for the ears on top of each other, right sides together. Following the line you traced in step 1, sew the curved line with a reduced stitch length. Cut out both ears with a 1/8" (3 mm) seam allowance. Cut the open side without seam allowance.

6. Turn both ears right side out. Use a pen or a wooden skewer to carefully push the fabric through the opening.

7. Stuff the ears with a little bit of polyfill stuffing. Fold the ears in half with the main fabric inside, and sew as shown in the figure. Make a seam 3/8" (1 cm) long, 1/4" (5 mm) from the folded center. Reopen the ears and press the small crease on the back with your fingers.

HEAD

8. Place the head (**10b**) wrong side up on the ironing board and put the cardstock shape (**10c**) on top, matching the design. Fold up the head seam allowance (marked in red on the pattern) over the shape, pressing with the tip of the iron.

9. Remove the cardstock and give it a good press on the right side, to make sure the edges are securely folded. Repeat all the steps for the second piece of the head.

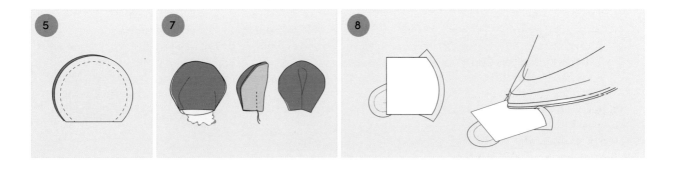

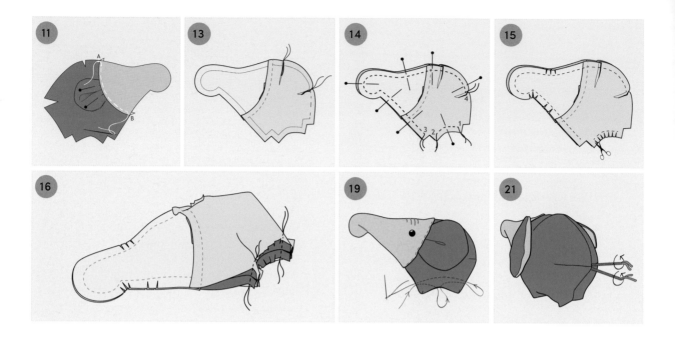

BODY

10. Pin the ears on the right side of the body (**10d**). Align the center of the ears using the reference mark on the body. You can sew the ears to the body to keep them in place.

11. Put the sides of the head on top of the corresponding sides of the body. Baste to match the AB line indicated on the pattern piece.

12. Topstitch close to the folded edge. Remove the basting.

13. Close the darts on the top of both sides of the body: pin the seam allowances of the slits, right sides together, and sew from the top of the slit to the raw edges of the fabric.

14. Put both sides of the elephant on top of each other, right sides together. Pin and sew from point 1 to point 2 and from point 3 to point 4 (see figure).

15. Clip the seam allowances as shown in the figure.

16. Fold the darts, close with some pins and then sew the darts on the front and rear paws, as shown in the figure.

17. Turn the elephant right side out. Use a wooden skewer to carefully push out the trunk. Stuff the elephant with polyfill stuffing. Use your fingers or a wooden skewer to reach the narrow parts of the elephant. Sew the opening by hand with a ladder stitch*.

18. Use a nylon thread to fix the two small beads at eyes' level, going through the head. Embroider the nose and some lines on the forehead with a topstitch thread.

19. Optional step to shape the legs:
Use another thread to pass between the paws as shown in the figure. Lightly pull the thread and knot the ends. Insert the two ends of the thread into a needle and hide them inside the body.

---

* see p. 10

20. Make the tail to finalize your elephant. Cut 6" (15 cm) of colored cotton thread. Double or triple the thread to obtain the right thickness for the tail. Thread a needle and pass it in and out at the point indicated for the tail: you'll get two tresses of the same length.

21. Twist the two tresses clockwise with the tips of your fingers. Twist them one by one and secure the ends so they don't loosen. Twist them very close while not loosening the tension on the threads. Then let them roll up around each other.

22. Tie a knot to finish the tail and cut the excess thread.

MEDIUM HOT AIR BALLOON WITH STARS, CLOUDS AND DROPS

The hot air balloon measures 6" (15 cm) in diameter.

● ● ●

WHAT YOU'LL NEED

- fabric glue
- polyfill stuffing
- wooden skewer (for turning)
- 2 clothespins
- cotton yarn for the hook
- thin cotton yarn
- cardstock
- 1/8" (3 mm) thick felt:
    6 6/8" x 2 3/8" (17 x 6 cm)
- plain and printed cotton fabric:
    4 pieces of 6 3/8" x 10" (16 x 25.5 cm) in
        different fabrics for the balloon
    6 6/8" x 5 1/8" (17 x 13 cm) for the top and
        the base of the balloon
    2 pieces of 6 1/8" x 3 5/8" (15.5 x 9 cm)
        in different fabrics for the stars
    2 pieces of 6 x 3 5/8" (15 x 9 cm) in different
        fabrics for the big cloud and a drop
    2 pieces of 4 6/8" x 3 5/8" (12 x 9 cm) in
        different fabrics for the small cloud and a drop

OPTIONAL

- fusible interfacing (as reinforcement if the fabric
  of your choice is very thin)
- fabric hole punch (to make holes in 3 mm thick
  felt, see step 22)
- tweezers (to stuff the stars and clouds with polyfill
  stuffing, see step 28)

CUTTING AND PREPARING THE MATERIAL

Read through the instructions before starting. Seam allowances are included in all pattern pieces where applicable.

Note

In this pattern I sometimes refer to the figures on p.25 of the big hot air balloon. The number of segments in these figures differ, but the action is exactly the same.

----

1. Trace two pieces of **segment (11a)** on the wrong side of four different fabrics. Cut out the eight pieces with a 1/4" (6 mm) seam allowance, as shown by the dotted line on the pattern piece.

2. Trace the **base ring (11b)**, the **base circle (11c)** and the **top circle (11d)** of the hot air balloon onto the wrong side of the fifth fabric. Cut out all the pieces with a 1/4" (6 mm) seam allowance as shown by the dotted line on the pattern piece.

3. Put the two fabrics you've chosen for the stars, clouds and drops on top of each other, right sides together. Trace the shapes of one **big star (11e)**, one **little star (11f)**, one **big cloud (11g)**, one **little cloud (11h)** and two **drops (11i)** onto the wrong side of one piece of cotton fabric, as shown in the figures.

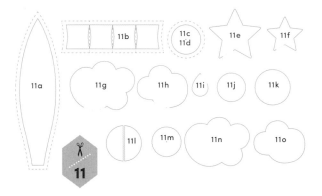

4. Trace one **reinforcement (11j)** and the **supports (11k)** and **(11l)** on a piece of 3 mm thick felt. Cut them without seam allowance.

5. Trace the shapes **top circle (11m)**, **big cloud (11n)** and **little cloud (11o)** onto a piece of cardstock and cut them.

BALLOON

6. Choose the sequence of the fabrics according to the color, for example light brown, brown, cream and yellow, repeated two times. Put the segments **(11a)** two by two on top of each other, right sides together, and sew them as shown in the figure.

    Important: The seams of the segments must follow the full lines drawn on the pattern piece as precisely as possible, so that the balloon will perfectly match the base. Do not sew through

the seam allowance up to the raw edge, but start from the x-point at the top of each segment.

Combine four segments at a time to make the two halves of the balloon.

7. To give the balloon a perfect shape, press the seam allowances between the segments open. Press as you go.

8. Put the two halves of the balloon on top of each other, right sides together. Pin carefully and sew them, leaving an opening of 5" (12 cm) on one side, as shown in figure 8 of the big hot air balloon (p. 25, the number of segments in this figure differs, but the action is exactly the same).

BASE OF THE BALLOON

9. Sew the darts of the base ring **(11b)** one by one. Fold the strip of fabric in half on the folding line, right sides together, and sew following the sewing line, as shown in figure 9 of the big hot air balloon (p. 25, the number of segments in this figure differs, but the action is exactly the same). Be careful not to sew through the seam allowance.

10. Close the base ring: fold the strip of fabric in half, right sides together, and sew half of the short side.

11. Put the base ring with the partly opened side seam downwards. Pin the circle **(11c)** to the open top of the base ring, right sides together, as shown in

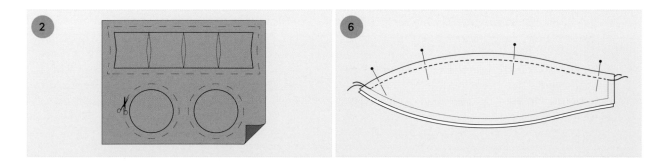

figure 11 of the big hot air balloon (p. 25, the number of segments in this figure differs, but the action is exactly the same). Sew with a seam allowance of 1/4" (6 mm). Turn the piece inside out.

12. Insert the base ring inside the balloon, right sides together. Pin the top of the ring together with the bottom of the balloon. Start at the opening in the side seam of both balloon and base. Align each crease of the base ring with the seams at every two color segments of the balloon, as shown in figure 12 of the big hot air balloon (p. 25, the number of segments in this figure differs, but the action is exactly the same). Carefully sew them together, using a seam allowance of 1/4" (6 mm).

13. Push the base of the balloon inside out. Pin and sew the open side of the base ring and 3/8" (10 mm) of the open side of the balloon, as shown in figure 13 of the big hot air balloon (p. 25, the number of segments in this figure differs, but the action is exactly the same). Keep the seam allowance between the ring and the balloon folded upward, in the direction of the balloon, while sewing.

14. Push the base ring inside the balloon until the seam allowance of the base circle is level with the opening in the balloon. Position the raw edges of the top and base circle together (the base ring is now folded in half, wrong sides together). Join the raw edges of the top and bottom of the base ring and sew them together to the balloon, as shown in figure 14 of the big hot air balloon (p. 25, the number of segments in this figure differs, but the action is exactly the same).

15. In this way, the base ring of the balloon – seen in the figure from the right side of the work – creates an edge that is deep enough to simulate the vacuum inside of a real hot air balloon. See figure 15 of the big hot air balloon (p. 25, the number of segments in this figure differs, but the result is the same).

REINFORCEMENT AT THE BASE OF THE BALLOON

16. Glue the felt reinforcement (**8j**) to the base, on the wrong side of the fabric circle, as shown in figure 16 of the big hot air balloon (p. 25, the number of segments in this figure differs, but the action is exactly the same). This will help shape the hot air balloon and give more stability to the bottom. Glue the seam allowance all around the piece of felt. Instead of gluing, you could also sew the circle by hand at the seam allowance of the bottom of the balloon, but glue will make your balloon sturdier.

TOP OF THE BALLOON

17. Cut three 12" (30 cm) pieces of cotton yarn to make the loop. Lock the pieces together with a clothespin on 3 7/8" (10 cm) from one end, make a braid of 2 3/8" (6 cm) and lock with a clothespin, leaving another 3 7/8" (10 cm) unbraided at the end. Fold the braid in half and knot the ends together, as also shown in figure 17 of the big hot air balloon (p. 25).

18. To finish the top of the balloon, lace a thread along the perimeter of the top circle (**11d**) and insert the cardstock shape (**11m**) on the wrong side into the fabric, as also shown in figure 18 of the big hot air balloon (p. 25). Pull and tie the two ends of the thread.

Note

Lacing can be done by hand, but you can also use the longest stitch length of your sewing machine, setting the thread tension at the minimum. Leave a long tail of thread at the beginning, sew all around the circle without backstitching neither at the start nor at the end, and use a long tail at the end as well.

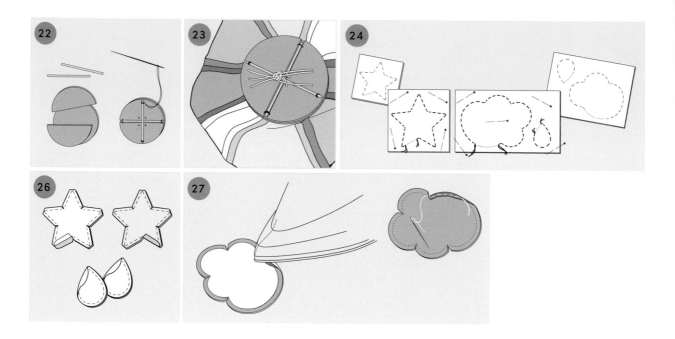

19. Iron the folded edge and remove the cardstock.

20. Pierce the center of the circle (**11d**) with a large needle and pass the ends of the hook one by one inside it.

21. Turn the balloon right side out. Insert the ends of the cotton yarn at the center top of the balloon, between the outer tips of the segments, as shown in figure 21 of the big hot air balloon (p. 25, the number of segments in this figure differs, but the action is exactly the same).

22. Take the two big circles of felt. Put the support (**11l**) on top of the support (**11k**) by matching the shapes. Take a wooden skewer and cut it into two sticks of 2" (5 cm) each. Insert one stick between the two parts of support (**11l**) and put the other stick on top to form a cross shape. Lock the sticks into place with some small stitches at the four ends of the sticks. Use a fabric hole punch or a large needle to make four holes in the felt, right next to the intersection of the sticks.

23. Turn the balloon inside out. Use a large needle to pass the yarn ends through the four holes in the felt. Securely tie the yarn ends above the intersection of the sticks, as shown in the figure. This method is really safe and makes sure the form of the hot air balloon will not change when you hang it. Turn the balloon right side out again.

STARS, CLOUDS AND DROPS

24. Cut out separate squares of fabric for each star, cloud and drop as shown in the figure. Pin the fabric layers together and sew carefully along the lines. Sew by machine or by hand with small stitches. Leave a section of the perimeter open, so you can turn the stars, the clouds and the drops right side out later on.

25. Cut out the stars and drops, leaving a 1/8" (3 mm) seam allowance (the seam allowance can be a little wider in the open area) and cut the tips and corners. Be very careful not to cut the seam. Cut out the clouds, leaving a 1 5/8" (5 mm) seam allowance and cut the corners.

26. Use the iron to fold the open seam allowance on each star and drop, as shown in the figure. This simple trick will make it easier to close the opening once the star is turned right side out.

27. Pressing the seam allowance of the clouds makes closing them easier. As this seam is curved, you can use a cardstock template to help you with the ironing. Take the cloud shapes (**11n**) and (**11o**) to bend the curved seam allowances more easily. Put a fabric cloud on the ironing board and put the corresponding shape on top, matching the design. Fold the open seam allowance of

the cloud over the cardstock, pressing with the tip of the iron. Iron the sides one after another. If necessary, lock the edges you have ironed into place with a couple of basting stitches.

28. Turn the stars, clouds and drops right side out. Push the fabric gently through the opening with a skewer. Be particularly careful with the little star. Stuff all the pieces. For the parts that are most difficult to reach, you can use tweezers to take very small amounts of polyfill stuffing and push them inside the shape.

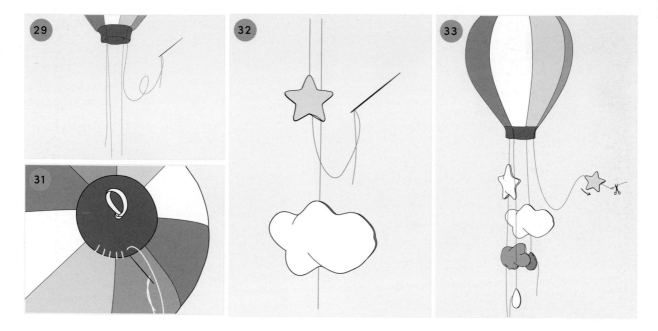

29. Now take the balloon and pass four cotton threads of 16" (40 cm) long through each crease of the base ring. Pass through the opening in the balloon to fix each cotton thread inside.

30. Stuff the balloon by pushing the stuffing inside. The balloon must be taut and firm. Close the opening by hand, between the segments.

31. Sew the fabric top circle with a cotton or top-stitching thread.

32. Hang the hot air balloon. Attach the stars and clouds to the cotton threads under the balloon. Pass the thread inside the stars with a needle and enter at the upper tip and out from the opening at the bottom. Do the same thing for the clouds, but enter at the center top point where the weight of the cloud is well-balanced.

33. Slide the stars and clouds along the threads to find a balanced composition. You can then lock

them in the chosen position. Measure the length between the base ring of the balloon and for example the tip of one star. Slide up the star and tie a knot in the thread at the distance you've measured. Then slide the star down again until you reach the knot, cut the surplus thread and hide it inside the star.

Lock the clouds in the same manner, then pass the thread back into the clouds and out from their center bottom point.

Attach one drop under each cloud. Pass the thread through the upper tip of the drop and out from the opening. Lock the drops in the chosen position, then cut the surplus thread and hide it inside.

Once you have fixed all the elements, you can remove the balloon from the hook and sew the openings of the stars, clouds and drops by hand. If the fabric is a little crumpled in the end, you can iron it, but without applying pressure.

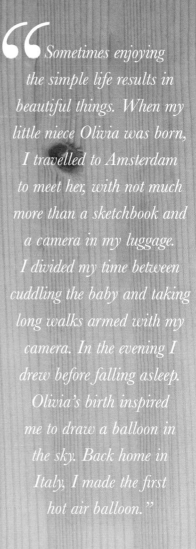

"Sometimes enjoying the simple life results in beautiful things. When my little niece Olivia was born, I travelled to Amsterdam to meet her, with not much more than a sketchbook and a camera in my luggage. I divided my time between cuddling the baby and taking long walks armed with my camera. In the evening I drew before falling asleep. Olivia's birth inspired me to draw a balloon in the sky. Back home in Italy, I made the first hot air balloon."

FLYING FOX

The fox is 16" (40.5 cm) long and 4 6/8" (12 cm) wide.

● ● ○

- -

WHAT YOU'LL NEED

- polyfill stuffing
- black cotton thread
- cardstock
- cream cotton fabric:
    5" x 3" (13 x 7 cm) for the front ears
- brown cotton fabric:
    3 1/8" x 1 3/8" (8 x 3.5 cm) for the nose
    4 pieces of 6 3/4" x 3 1/8" (17 x 8 cm) for
        the paws
- orange cotton fabric:
    6 3/4" x 3 3/4" (17 x 9.5 cm) for the snout
    6 3/4" x 9" (17 x 23 cm) for the back body
    6 3/4" x 4 1/8" (17 x 10.5 cm) for the front body
    2 pieces of 2 3/8" x 3 1/2" (6 x 9 cm) for
        the tail base
- brown pile or soft fabric:
    9" x 3 1/8" (23 x 8 cm) for the back ears
- cream pile or soft fabric:
    2 pieces of 6 3/4" x 4 3/8" (17 x 11 cm) for
        the head
    6 3/4" x 17 3/8" (17 x 44 cm) for the belly
    2 pieces of 2 3/8" x 11 3/8" (6 x 29 cm) for
        the tail

CUTTING AND PREPARING THE MATERIAL

Read through the instructions before starting. Seam allowances are included in all pattern pieces where applicable.

1. Put the two rectangles of cotton fabric for the nose and the snout on top of each other, right sides together. Center and align the longest sides. Pin and sew them 1/4" (6 mm) from the edge. Press the seam allowances open.

2. Trace the **snout (12a)** onto the wrong side of the fabric piece, making sure to align the upper line on the nose with the seam. Cut out the snout with a 1/4" (6 mm) seam allowance, as shown by the dotted line on the pattern piece.

3. Trace two pieces of the **head (12b)** onto the wrong side of the cream pile. Cut out the pieces with a 1/4" (6 mm) seam allowance, as shown by the dotted line on the pattern piece.

4. Trace two mirrored **back ears (12c)** onto the wrong side of the brown pile. Cut them with a 1/4" (6 mm) seam allowance.

5. Trace two **front ears (12d)** onto the wrong side of a cream cotton fabric. Cut them with a 1/4" (6 mm) seam allowance.

6. Take one rectangle of fabric for the paws and the rectangle for the front body. Put them on top of each other, right sides together. Align the 6 3/4" (17 cm) sides, pin and sew them together at 1/4" (6 mm) from the edge. Press the seam allowances open. Trace the **forepaws (12e)** onto the wrong side of the fabric piece, making sure to align the paws line with the seam. Cut out the forepaws with a 1/4" (6 mm) seam allowance, as shown by the dotted line on the pattern piece.

7. Sew together another rectangle of fabric for the paws and the rectangle for the back body, as described in step 6. Trace the **back body (12f)** onto the wrong side of the fabric piece, making sure to align the paws line with the seam. Cut out the back body with a 1/4" (6 mm) seam allowance, as shown by the dotted line on the pattern piece.

8. Place the pile rectangle for the belly on a flat surface. Put the two remaining rectangles for the paws on top of it, right sides together. Align the long edge of the cotton fabrics with the red lines marked on the pattern piece (**12g**), as shown in the picture. Pin and sew the layers of

pile and cotton along these sides 1/4" (6 mm) from the raw edge. (Check image 9 to see the result.) If you're having difficulties to maintain the right seam allowance because the marks on your machine are hidden by the fabric, you can mark the sewing line on the fabric before sewing (blue line on the pattern piece).

9. Fold the rectangles of cotton towards the paws.

10. Trace the perimeter of the **belly (12g)** onto the wrong side of the fabric, making sure to align the paw lines with the seams. Pin both fabrics together to make sure they don't move while cutting, and cut out the belly with a 1/4" (6 mm) seam al-

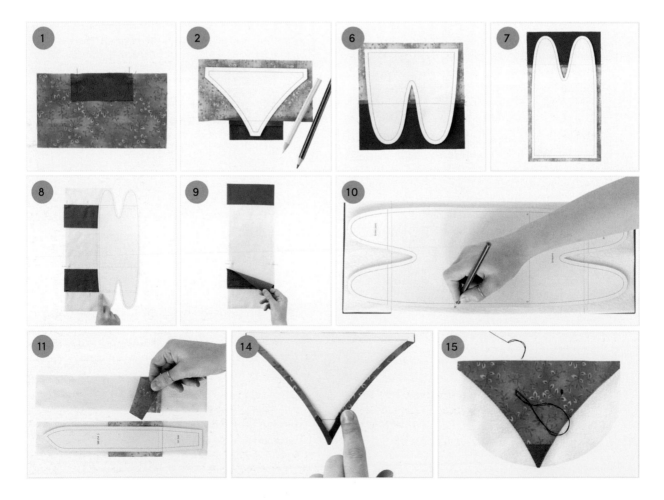

lowance, as shown by the dotted line on the pattern piece. Mark the points A and B on the wrong side of the fabric.

11. Take the two rectangles of cream pile and orange cotton you've prepared for the tail. Put the cotton for the base of the tail on top of the pile, right sides together. Align the short edge with the mark on the pattern piece (**12h),** as shown in the picture. Pin and sew the layers of fabric along this edge 1/4" (6 mm) from the raw edge. If you're having difficulties to maintain the right seam allowance because the marks on your machine are hidden by the fabric, you can mark the sewing line on the fabric before sewing (black line on the pattern piece). Fold the rectangles of cotton toward the bottom of the tail.

12. Trace the **tail** (**12h**) onto the wrong side of one piece of fabric, making sure to align the line of the tail base with the seam. Don't cut yet!

13. Trace the **snout shape** (**12i**) and the **body shape** (**12j**) onto a piece of cardstock and cut.

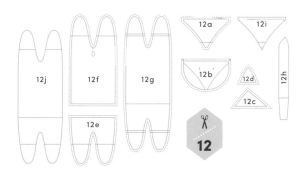

SNOUT

14. Fold the side edges of the snout over the shape (**12i**), as shown in the picture. Put the cardstock on the wrong side of the fabric, matching the design of the snout, and iron the edges.

15. Put the snout on top of the upper head, right side of the fabrics facing up, and pin it in place. Topstitch close to the folded edges of the snout, changing the color of thread according to the fabric. For a very neat result, do not backstitch by machine when you change between brown and orange, but lace the loose ends to the wrong side of the fabric and secure them by hand. Embroider the eyes with a black cotton thread, as shown in the picture. Secure the loose ends on the wrong side of the fabric.

16. Put the front and back sides of the ears on top of each other, right sides together. Pin and sew the ears along the right and left edges, one at a time, as shown in the picture.

17. Cut the corners and turn the ears right side out. Use a wooden skewer to carefully push out the tips.

18. Stuff the ears a little bit with some polyfill stuffing and pin the opening, aligning the edges. Sew the ears near the bottom edge and cut the surplus of fabric. Make sure to sew with a sewing allowance as small as possible to avoid that this seam is visible in the end result.

HEAD

19. Place the ears over the upper head between the points A and B, as shown in the picture. The ears

are slightly overlapping at the center of the head. Pin and sew the pieces together near the head top edge. Make sure to sew with a seam allowance as small as possible to avoid that this seam is visible in the end result.

20. Put the upper head on top of the back body (**12f**) and the bottom head on top of the forepaws (**12e**), right sides together, by matching the AB line. Pin and sew both pieces at 1/4" (6 mm) from the edge.

    Important: The seams must follow the full line drawn on the pattern piece exactly from point A to B. Do not sew through the seam allowance up to the raw edge. Catch the seam you made in step 19, to make sure it's not visible after turning.

21. Unfold the two pieces you've just sewn and put them on top of each other, right sides together. Pin making sure the seams are aligned and sew the round edge of the upper and bottom head, using a seam allowance of 1/4" (6 mm), and sew exactly from point A to point B.

BODY

22. Keeping the head wrong side out, unfold the forepaws of the piece you've just sewn. Put it on top of the belly (**12g**) by matching the AB line, right sides together. Pin all around the back body and the forepaws with the belly piece, making sure to align the seams of the paws.

23. Carefully sew first along the perimeter of the forepaws and then all around the back body, 1/4" (6 mm) from the edge. Leave a section of the perimeter open, as shown in the pattern, so you can turn the fox right side out later on. Always sew from point A to point B, no further than this. To make it easier to follow the rounded seams between the legs of the fox, you can use the body shape (**12j**) to mark them on the wrong side of the fabric.

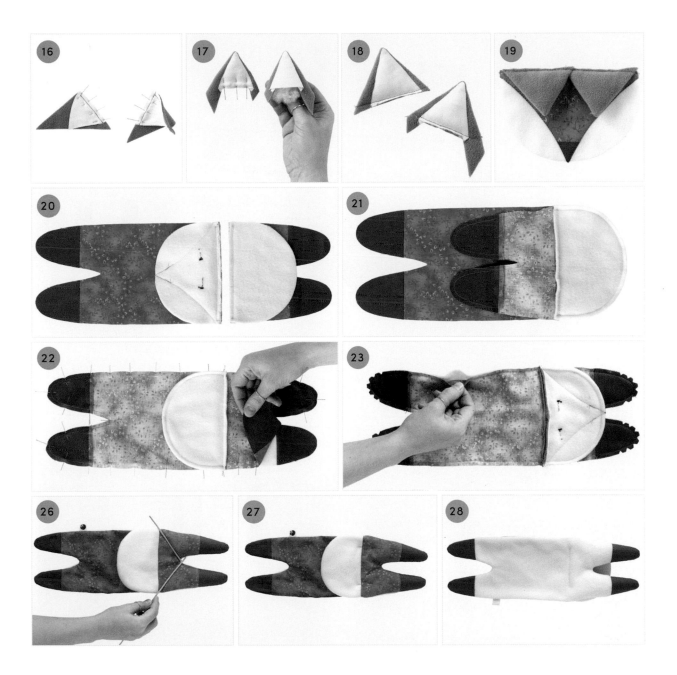

24. Clip the seam allowance between the paws of the fox and notch the curved edges.

25. Turn the fox right side out. First turn the ears and the head, then the paws and the body.

26. Stuff the forepaws of the fox up until the lines shown in the picture.

27/28.
Pin and close the forepaws along the AB line by machine. Leave 1" (2.5 cm) on both sides of the seam free, as shown in the pictures.

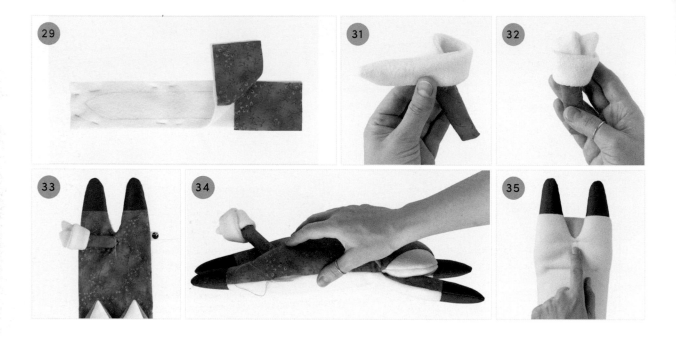

29. Put the two sides of the tail on top of each other, right sides together, making sure to match the seams between the two kinds of fabric. Sew all around following the outline you traced in step 12 onto one wrong side, except the edge at the base. (The tail will be turned through the base. If your fabric is very stiff or thick, it might be useful to leave an opening for turning at the side of the tail.)

30. Cut out the seam allowance to 1/8" (3 mm). Turn the tail right side out using a wooden skewer.

31/32.

Tie a knot to the tail as shown in the pictures. Fold 3/8" (1 cm) of the open edge inwards.

33. Mark the tail area onto the back body. Sew the tail in place, all around the folded base, by hand. Tie the thread inside the body and cut the loose ends.

34. Stuff the fox with small amounts of polyfill stuffing at a time. First stuff the head and the rear paws, then the body. Sew the opening by hand.

35. Pin and sew the center point of the forepaws together with the bottom head piece.

"I love to inspire people to discover or refine the love of handcrafting. In Italy, the interest in crafting has been a bit lost over time, although recently many people have rediscovered the value of unique, handmade things, constructed with both dedication and time. Especially in the north of Italy, there are many artisans and people who appreciate the value of handicrafts. It's heartwarming to know fans from all over the world are inspired by my creations."

RABBIT BOOKEND

The rabbit is 9 5/8" (24.5 cm) tall.

●●○

- -

WHAT YOU'LL NEED

- a stitching awl or a large embroidery needle with a pointed end
- masking tape / transparent adhesive tape
- topstitch thread
- cardstock
- polyfill stuffing
- 2 little screws for the eyes ø about 1/4" (5 mm). Use safety eyes if the rabbit book end is intended for small kids.
- screwdriver
- a plastic bag
- thin sand
- faux leather, possibly matt, soft to the touch and non-stretchable:
    16" x 11" (40 x 28 cm) for the body
    1 3/8" x 1 6/8" (3.5 x 4.5 cm) for the nose
- 1/8" (3 mm) thick felt:
    4 2/8" x 5 1/8" (11 x 13 cm)
- 3/4" (20 mm) polyfill fiber sheet:
    8" x 11" (20 x 27.5 cm)

OPTIONAL

- tweezers (to stuff the ears with the polyfill fiber sheet, see step 22)

Note

- -

It's important to choose a matching color for the thread, both for normal seams and topstitching. The material is stiffer then fabric, so the thread will always be visible in the seams.

- -

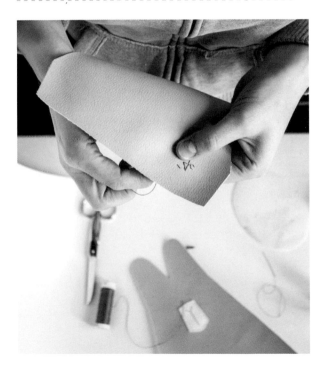

CUTTING AND PREPARING THE MATERIAL

Read through the instructions before starting. Seam allowances are included in all pattern pieces where applicable.

1. If you have a steady hand, trace the pattern pieces to carbon paper. Alternatively, you can photocopy the pieces. There are a lot of exact points to transfer onto the faux leather, which makes it hard to trace it by hand. Glue the copied pieces on a piece of cardstock and carefully cut out all the pieces of cardstock along the cutting line. These will now be used to trace each rabbit shape on the faux leather. Place the **front (13a)**, the **back (13b)**, the **nose (13c)** and the **base (13d)** on the right side of the faux leather. Use masking tape between the cardstock and the pieces of faux leather to fix them together (check first to make sure the tape doesn't damage the material).

2/3.

Take a large embroidery needle with a pointed end or a stitching awl and transfer all of the dots from the pattern piece onto the faux leather. Put a piece of cardstock or other suitable material under the faux leather to avoid damaging the table top and the needle tip. The transferred points on the faux leather will help you to make perfect seams.

4/5.

Trace the outline of all parts of the rabbit on the faux leather with a pen.

6/7.

Remove the cardstock shapes and cut out each piece drawn on the faux leather exactly along the inside of the traced outline, as shown in the picture. When cutting, be sure to completely remove the pen mark, so that you will get shapes identical to the pattern pieces.

8. Use the **body shape (13e)** to mark the lines to sew by machine on the wrong side of one piece of the rabbit's body.

9. Cut out the same body shape (**13e**) once from a 20 mm polyfill fiber sheet.

10. Trace one **base reinforcement (13f)** on the felt and two identical pieces on a piece of cardstock. Cut them out along the marked line. Also prepare two little felt pieces of 7/8" x 3/8" (2 x 1 cm) to use later behind the eyes.

11. Glue the two pieces of cardstock together, and then glue the felt base on top of the cardstock. Set the base reinforcement aside to dry.

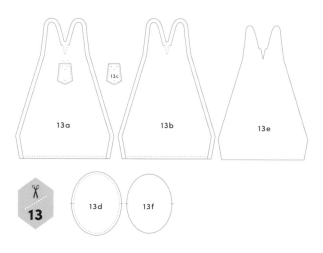

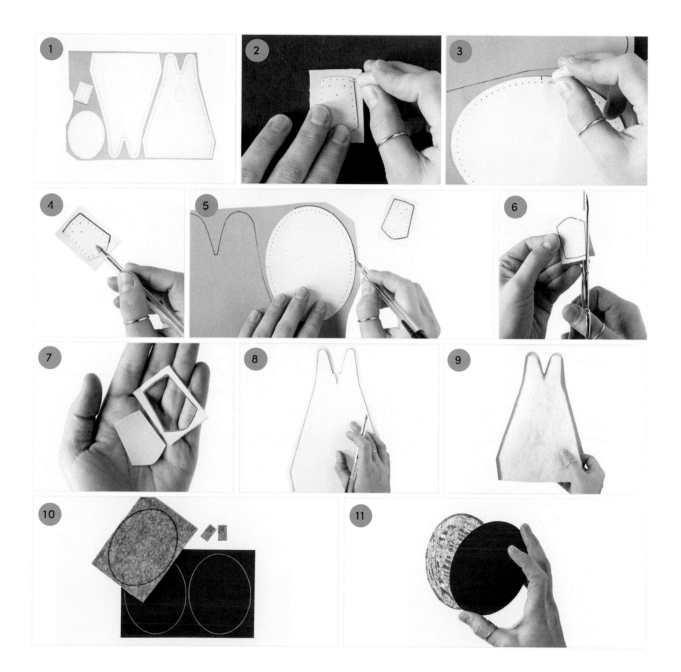

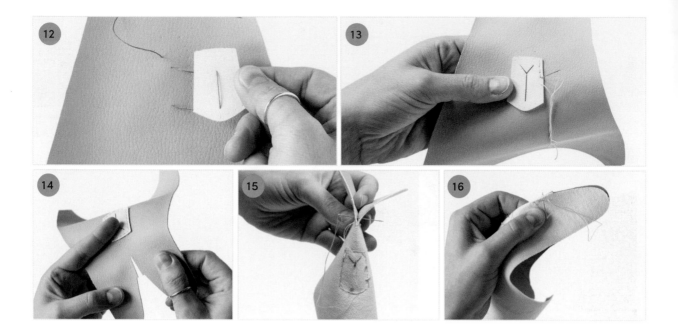

NOSE

12. Place the nose (**13c**) on the front (**13a**) of the rabbit, with the right sides of the two pieces of faux leather facing upwards. Align the points impressed in the faux leather and embroider the nose combining the three central points with a colored topstitch thread (about 8" - 20 cm): check image 13 to see the result. Tie the thread on the back and cut the loose ends.

13. Sew the perimeter of the nose with 20" (50 cm) of topstitch thread, exactly following the dots impressed on the faux leather. Tie the thread on the wrong side and cut the loose ends.

HEAD

14. Cut a slit in the faux leather on the forehead of the rabbit, between the two lines of dots, as shown in the picture.

15/16.

Fold the rabbit's head in half, right sides together, and sew the crease on the forehead following the dots marked on the faux leather. Sew from the bottom to the top of the crease and back. Tie the thread and cut the loose ends. Repeat steps 14 to 16 for the crease at the back of the head.

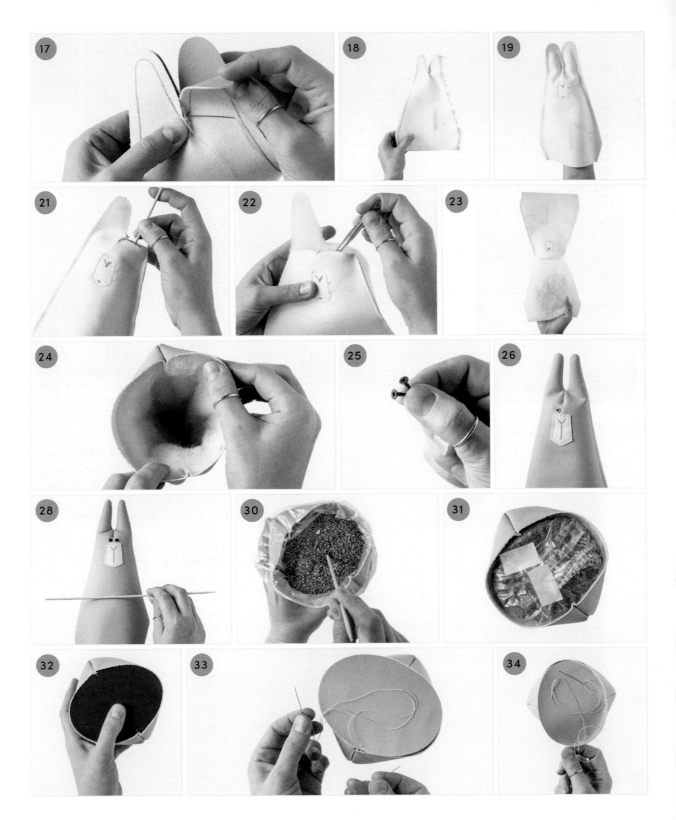

17. Put the front and the back of the rabbit on top of each other, right sides together. Lock the two sides of the head with a hand stitch exactly in the middle, to make sure the two layers of faux leather don't move at this point during the following steps.

18. Pin the two layers of faux leather together along one side of the body. Pin within the seam allowance and make sure not to damage the right visible side of the faux leather.

19. Sew by machine along the line drawn on the back of one piece of the body, exactly from the center point on the head to the rabbit's base or in the opposite direction. Remove the pins as you proceed with the seam. Pin and sew the other side of the body in the same way.

20. Trim the seam allowances by half and clip the faux leather in the corners.

21. Gently push the ears of the rabbit inside the head with a wooden skewer.

22. Insert the ears of the polyfill shape into the ears of faux leather, as shown in the picture. Use tweezers or a wooden skewer to push them until they reach the tip of the ears.

23. Divide the polyfill sheet into two layers, creating a bag, without separating the edges at the sides. This additional layer on the inside of the rabbit allows you to create a uniform surface on the outside of the bookends and hides the dividing line between the soft polyfill stuffing and the sand.

24. Gently turn the rabbit right side out while including the polyfill shape inside it.

25/26.

Take two little screws for the eyes. Insert one hand inside the rabbit and place the two rectangles of felt under the area of the eyes, on top of each other. Carefully screw the eyes at the marked dots, taking care not to damage the faux leather.

27. Stuff the rabbit by pressing the stuffing inside. Start by pushing a bit of polyfill stuffing in the ears with a wooden skewer.

28. Stuff half of the body, up to the line shown in the picture.

29. Insert a plastic bag inside the bottom of the body and pour in the sand, little by little. Sit down and keep the rabbit between your legs or put it in a deep glass to keep it upright during the next steps.

30. Repeatedly poke the sand with a stick to fill any empty spaces, being careful not to break the bag. Fill the rabbit almost to the top. The sand should be firmly pressed together.

31. Cut the plastic bag until there's about 2" (5 cm) left from the bottom side of the rabbit. Bend the edges toward the center of the body to close the bag, being careful not to pull it out of shape. Secure the edges with a piece of transparent adhesive tape.

32. Put the base reinforcement (**13f**) on top of the plastic bag, with the felt side facing the bottom of the rabbit. (The felt side is on the inside and the cardstock is on the outside.) Match the mark on the reinforcement with the sides of the body.

33. Put the faux leather base (**13d**) on top of the base reinforcement, matching the shapes. Cut 35" (90 cm) of topstitching thread and sew the base of faux leather to the rabbit's body, wrong sides together. Start sewing from one side of the rabbit. Pass the thread halfway through a point on the body and the corresponding point on the base. Thread a needle onto each end of the thread.

34. Sew the seam a little at a time by alternating the use of both needles. Follow the points impressed on the faux leather to obtain a perfect topstitch on both sides of the work. Once you've sewn along the entire perimeter, tie and cut the threads.

MR. HEDGEHOG – KEYCHAIN, PINCUSHION, PENDANT, LUCKY CHARM

The hedgehog is 3 1/4" (8 cm) tall, 5" (12.5 cm) long and 2 3/8" (6 cm) wide.

● ● ○

WHAT YOU'LL NEED

- polyfill stuffing
- wooden skewer (for turning)
- cardstock
- plain and printed cotton fabric:
    3 1/8" x 3 1/8" (8 x 8 cm) for the ears
    5" x 3" (13 x 8 cm) for the head
    9 1/2" x 5" (25 x 13 cm) for the body
- waxed cord 5" (13 cm)

OPTIONAL

- woven fusible interfacing (as reinforcement if the fabric of your choice is very thin)
- nylon thread ø .008" (0.20 mm)

CUTTING AND PREPARING THE MATERIAL

Read through the instructions before starting. Seam allowances are included in all pattern pieces where applicable.

1. Cut one fabric square of 3 1/8" (8 cm) wide for the ears.

2. Trace two mirrored patterns of the **body (14b)** onto the wrong side of the fabric. Cut out the pieces with a 1/4" (6 mm) seam allowance, as shown by the dotted line on the pattern piece.

3. Cut a piece of cardstock with the **shape (14c)** drawn in the pattern.

4. Trace two patterns of the **head (14d)** onto the wrong side of the fabric. Draw the reference mark for the ears. Cut out the pieces with a 1/4" (6 mm) seam allowance, as shown by the dotted line on the pattern piece.

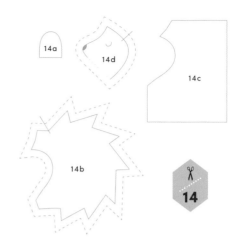

EARS

5. Fold the square fabric right sides together, to create a rectangle. Trace two patterns of the **ear (14a)** on the wrong side of the fabric as shown in the figure. Sew the curved lines. Cut out both ears **(14a)** with a 1/8" (3 mm) seam allowance. Cut the open side without seam allowance. Turn the ears right side out. Use a wooden skewer to carefully push the fabric through the opening.

6. Fold the two ears in half and sew as shown in the figure, in the middle between the fold and the outer edge. Open the ears and press with your fingers on the small crease on the back.

BODY

7. Clip into the seam allowance of the two body pieces in the inward curve. The small cuts should only be 1/8" (3 mm) deep.

8. Place one fabric piece of the body wrong side up on the ironing board and put the cardstock shape on top, matching the design.

9. Fold the body seam allowance (marked in red on the pattern piece) over the cardstock shape, pressing with the tip of the iron. Remove the cardstock shape and give it a good press from the right side, to make sure the edges are securely folded under.

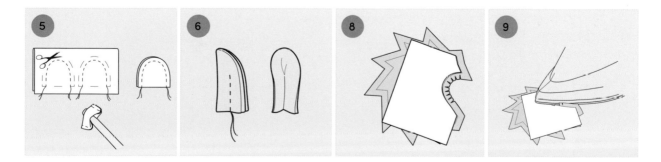

10. Baste the edge of the inward curve.
Repeat steps 8, 9 and 10 for the other side of the body.

HEAD

11. Pin the ears on the right side of the head pieces as shown in the figure. Align the center of the ears with the mark on the head, and make sure that the raw edge extends over the raw edge of the head by about 1/8" (3 mm).

PUT ALL THE PIECES TOGETHER

12. Put the sides of the body on top of each corresponding side of the head. Baste along the AB line, indicated on the pattern piece. Topstitch close to the folded edge and remove the basting.

13. If you want to make a keychain, pin the waxed cord on the right side of one of the hedgehog's body pieces, otherwise skip this step.

14. Put the two sides of the hedgehog on top of each other, right sides together. Pin and sew all around, leaving the bottom side of the head open.

Cut off the excess fabric of the ears and the seam allowances as shown in the figure. Make a knot at the end of the waxed cord. Trim and clip the seam allowance.

15. Turn the hedgehog right side out. Use a wooden skewer to carefully push out the spines.

16. Take very small amounts of polyfill stuffing and push them in each spine with the help of a wooden skewer. Stuff the rest of the hedgehog with polyfill stuffing, making sure to fill the center of the body very firmly, to give the hedgehog a nice and rounded shape. Fold the ears towards the head while stuffing: by firmly stuffing the body with the ears fixed in this position, the stuffing will keep the seam allowance inside the head in the opposite direction, which will give the ears the right position in the end result.

17. Embroider the eyes and the nose with black thread, hiding the knots inside the head. Sew the opening of the head by hand.

18. Attach a key ring to the waxed cord and Mr. Hedgehog is ready!

"I put a lot of thought in the preliminary study of a pattern. I visualize and draw not only the finished object, but also all the steps to get there. This allows me to discover bottlenecks quickly and reach my goal faster: it's a sort of invisible test. Few designs were perfect on the first try, and I know that perfectionism is my Achilles heel, but I rarely need more than two or three test models. The polar bear took me the most versions. Some of the tests became gifts — my mother is an enthusiastic foster mother of my work — and others remain in my workspace as study objects, precisely because of their ugliness."

SMALL HOT AIR BALLOON WITH BASKET AND STARS

The hot air balloon measures 4" (10 cm) in diameter.

• • •

WHAT YOU'LL NEED

- fabric glue
- polyfill stuffing
- large needle
- cardboard
- clothespins
- cotton yarn for the hook
- thin cotton yarn
- 1/8" (3 mm) thick felt:
    4 4/8" x 2" (11.5 x 5 cm)
- plain and printed cotton fabric:
    4 pieces of 5" x 7" (13 x 18 cm) in different
        fabrics for the balloon
    5" x 4" (13 x 10 cm) for the top and the base
        of the balloon
    5" x 5" (13 x 13 cm) for the basket
    2 pieces of 5 4/8" x 5 4/8" (14 x 14 cm) for stars

OPTIONAL

- fusible interfacing (as reinforcement if the fabric
  of your choice is very thin)
- fabric hole punch (to make holes in 3 mm thick
  felt and cardstock, see step 22)
- tweezers (to stuff the stars with polyfill stuffing,
  see step 33)

Note

----
*In this pattern I sometimes refer to the figures on p.25 of
the big hot air balloon. The number of segments in these
figures differ, but the action is exactly the same.*

CUTTING AND PREPARING THE MATERIAL

Read through the instructions before starting. Seam allowances are included in all pattern pieces where applicable.

1. Trace two pieces of **segment (15a)** on the wrong side of four different fabrics. Cut out the eight pieces with a 1/4" (6 mm) seam allowance, as shown by the dotted line in the pattern.

2. Trace the **base ring (15b)**, the **base circle (15c)** and the **top circle (15d)** of the hot air balloon onto the wrong side of the fifth fabric. Cut out all the pieces with a 1/4" (6 mm) seam allowance as shown by the dotted line on the pattern piece.

3. Trace one **basket side (15e)**, one **bottom base (15f)** and one **top base (15g)** onto the wrong side of the fabric you've chosen for the basket. Cut out all the pieces with a 1/4" (6mm) seam allowance, except for the top base.

4. Put the fabrics you've chosen for the stars on top of each other, wrong sides together. Trace the shapes of four **stars (15h)** onto the right side of one piece of cotton fabric, as shown in figure 31.

5. Trace one **support** (**15i**), one **reinforcement** (**15j**) and one **base basket** (**15k**) on a piece of 3 mm thick felt and one **support** (**15l**) on a piece of cardboard. Cut all the circles without seam allowance. Trace the shape **top circle** (**15m**) onto a piece of cardboard and cut it.

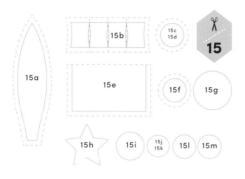

BALLOON

6. Choose the sequence of the fabrics according to the color, for example light brown, pink, cream and brown, repeated two times. Put the segments (**15a**) two by two on top of each other, right sides together, and sew them as shown in the figure.

Important: The seams of the segments must follow the full lines drawn on the pattern piece as precisely as possible, so that the balloon will perfectly match the base. Do not sew through the seam allowance up to the raw edge, but start from the x-point at the top of each segment.

Combine four segments at a time to make the two halves of the balloon.

7. To give the balloon a perfect shape, press the seam allowances between the segments open. Press as you go.

8. Put the two halves of the balloon on top of each other, right sides together. Pin carefully and sew them, leaving an opening of 3" (8 cm) on one side, as shown in figure 8 of the big hot air balloon (p. 25, the number of segments in this figure differs, but the action is exactly the same).

BASE OF THE BALLOON

9. Sew the darts of the base ring (**15b**) one by one. Fold the strip of fabric in half on the folding line, right sides together, and sew following the sewing line, as shown in figure 9 of the big hot air balloon (p. 25, the number of segments in this figure differs, but the action is exactly the same). Be careful not to sew through the seam allowance.

10. Close the base ring: fold the strip of fabric in half, right sides together, and sew half of the short side.

11. Put the base ring with the partly opened side seam downwards. Pin and baste the circle (**15c**) together with the open top of the base ring, right sides together, as shown in figure 11 of the big hot air balloon (p. 25, the number of segments in this figure differs, but the action is exactly the same). Sew with a seam allowance of 1/4" (6 mm). Turn the piece inside out.

12. Insert the base ring inside the balloon, right sides together. Pin and baste the top of the ring to the bottom of the balloon. Start at the opening in the side seam of both balloon and base. Align each crease of the base ring with the seams at every two color segments of the balloon, as shown in figure 12 of the big hot air balloon (p. 25, the number of segments in this figure differs, but the action is exactly the same). Carefully sew them together, using a seam allowance of 1/4" (6 mm).

13. Push the base of the balloon inside out. Pin and sew the open side of the base ring and 3/8" (10 mm) of the open side of the balloon, as shown in figure 13 of the big hot air balloon (p. 25, the number of segments in this figure differs, but the action is exactly the same). Keep the seam allowance between the ring and the balloon folded upward, in the direction of the balloon, while sewing.

14. Push the base ring inside the balloon until the seam allowance of the base circle is level with the opening in the balloon. Position the raw edges of the top and base circle together (the base ring is now folded in half, wrong sides together). You can see the end result in figure 15 of the big hot air balloon. Join the raw edges of the top and bottom of the base ring and sew them together to the balloon, as shown in figure 14 of the big hot air balloon (p. 25, the number of segments in this figure differs, but the action is exactly the same).

15. In this way, the base ring of the balloon – seen in the figure from the right side of the work – creates an edge that is deep enough to simulate the vacuum inside of a real hot air balloon. See figure 15 of the big hot air balloon (p. 25, the number of segments in this figure differs, but the result is the same).

REINFORCEMENT AT THE BASE OF THE BALLOON

16. Glue the felt reinforcement (**15j**) to the base, on the wrong side of the fabric circle, as shown in figure 16 of the big hot air balloon (p. 25, the number of segments in this figure differs, but the action is exactly the same). This will help shape the hot air balloon, as well as give more stability to the bottom of the balloon. Glue the seam allowance all around the piece of felt. Instead of gluing, you could also sew the circle by hand at the seam allowance of the bottom of the balloon, but glue will make your balloon sturdier.

TOP OF THE BALLOON

17. Cut three 12" (30 cm) pieces of cotton yarn to make the loop. Lock the pieces together with a clothespin on 3 7/8" (10 cm) from one end, make a braid of 2 3/8" (6 cm) and lock with a clothespin, leaving another 3 7/8" (10 cm) unbraided at the end. Fold the braid in half and knot the ends together, as also shown in figure 17 of the big hot air balloon (p. 25).

18. To finish the top of the balloon, lace a thread along the perimeter of the top circle (**15d**) and insert the cardstock shape (**15m**) on the wrong side into the fabric, as also shown in figure 18 of the big hot air balloon (p. 25). Pull and tie the two ends of the thread.

Note

Lacing can be done by hand, but you can also use the longest stitch length of your sewing machine, setting the thread tension at the minimum. Leave a long tail of thread at the beginning, sew all around the circle without backstitching neither at the start nor at the end, and use a long tail at the end too.

19. Iron the folded edge and remove the cardstock.

20. Pierce the center of the circle with a large needle and pass the ends of the hook one by one inside it.

21. Turn the balloon right side out. Insert the ends of the cotton yarn at the center top of the balloon, between the outer tips of the segments, as shown in figure 21 of the big hot air balloon (p. 25, the number of segments in this figure differs, but the action is exactly the same).

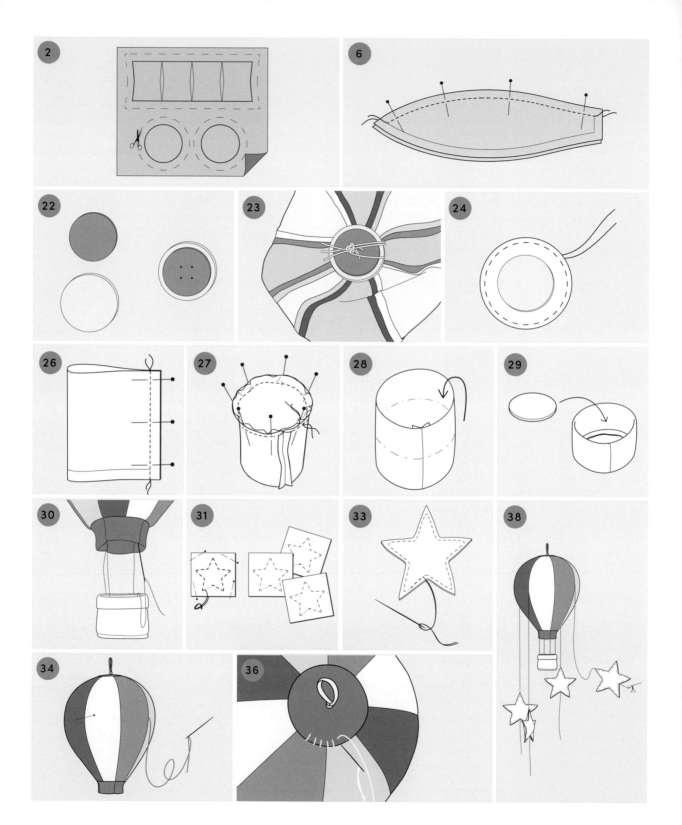

22. Put the support circles of felt (**15i**) and cardboard (**15l**) on top of each other. Glue them together. Use a fabric hole punch or a large needle to make four holes in the center of the support, as shown in the figure.

23. Turn the balloon inside out. Use a large needle to pass the yarn ends through the four holes in the felt. Securely tie the yarn above the center of the cardstock piece, as shown in the figure. This method is really safe and makes sure the form of the hot air balloon will not change when you hang it. Turn the balloon right side out again.

BASKET

24. Lace a thread along the perimeter of the top base (**15g**) and insert the felt base basket (**15k**) into the fabric on the wrong side.

25. Pull and tie the two ends of the thread, including the felt circle into the fabric.

26. Fold the basket side (**15e**) in half, right sides together, and sew the short edge, as shown in the figure. Press the seam allowance open.

27. Pin and baste the bottom base (**15f**) to one open edge of the basket, right sides together. Sew with a seam allowance of 1/4" (6 mm). Turn the piece right side out.

28. Fold half of the open edge inward.

29. Glue the top base inside the basket, wrong side down. Press the circle piece well onto the seam allowances. Bend the edge of the basket slightly outward (about 3/8" - 8 mm).

30. Use a thin cotton yarn to connect the basket to the base of the hot air balloon. Pass a needle under the edge to tie one end of the cotton yarn to a point of the basket. Insert the needle into the fold of the ring and pass along one crease until you reach the inside of the balloon. Adjust the length of the yarn so that the basket hangs about 2 2/8" (3 cm) under the balloon. Lock the yarn inside the balloon. Do this for three other points at equal distances on the top of the basket.

STARS

31. Cut out separate squares of fabric for each star as shown in the figure. Pin the fabric layers together and sew carefully along the line. Sew by machine or by hand with small stitches. Leave a section of the perimeter open to fill the stars.

32. Cut out the stars, leaving a 1/8" (3 mm) seam allowance.

33. Stuff all the stars. For the parts that are most difficult to reach, you can use tweezers to take very small amounts of stuffing and push them inside the shape. Sew the opening of the four stars by hand.

34. Now take the balloon and mark it with pins at every two segments and at 3" (7.5 cm) from the center top. Pass four cotton threads of 14" (35 cm) long through the points you've marked to hang the stars. Pass through the opening in the balloon to fix each cotton thread inside.

35. Stuff the balloon by pushing the stuffing inside. The balloon must be taut and firm. Close the opening by hand, between the segments.

36. Sew the fabric top circle with a cotton or topstitching thread.

37. Hang the hot air balloon. Attach the stars to the cotton threads all around the balloon. Pass the thread inside the stars with a needle and enter at the upper tip and out from the center point at the bottom.

38. Slide the stars along the threads to find a balanced composition. You can then lock them in the chosen position. Measure the length between the balloon and the center bottom of each star. Slide up the stars and tie a knot in the thread at the distance you've measured. Then slide the stars down again until you reach the knots, hiding the knots in the star's seam allowance. Cut the surplus thread and secure the knots with a little drop of glue. If the fabric is a little crumpled in the end, you can iron it, but without applying pressure.

Thank you!

Being a part of this project is a dream come true for me, so I sunk in my teeth from the first moment. It turned 2016 into a busy year: while gathering scraps and patches to make the right composition for my designs, I was scraping free hours together to compose this book the way I wanted. It took quite a bit of effort, but also brought me a lot of joy, and it was absolutely worth it!

I want to thank the wonderful team of Meteoor Books for believing in me and inviting me on this exciting adventure. Thank you also to the testers who helped proofread the patterns for this book.

A big thank you for my parents, they strongly believe in what I do and they like what I make. I can count on them to help me when it's hard, and when things work out, they're in for the celebrations as well. My partner Giordano is the best support ever, even when the scale between my time for him and my time for work wasn't always equally balanced.

My friends make a good team, showing me trust and affection, encouraging me with or without words. Many thanks to all of you!

Also thanks to those who follow me and appreciate my work unconditionally: I don't know you in person, but you keep me going!

But the biggest thanks is always for my grandmother Lea, my second mom. She lives in my heart, in my memories, in my hands and in the instruments that she made me love. She is always with me between the thimble, the needles and the fabrics ...

Thanks,

Vanessa Behymer

Libby Sharp

Narelle Heath

Tiffany Zelenga

Deborah Zaleski

Bianca Dewamme

Fenna Bredenhof

Melanie Call

Marie-Eve Miousse

Jess DeWit

Patti McCarry

Mary Ito

Riet Van de Walle

Ervyna Ahmad

Kir Vanhees

Examples made by
proofreaders using
patterns from this book.
Share your pictures on
Instagram with
#myhandmadeworld
and #johandmadedesignpattern

Copyright © 2017 Meteoor bvba
My handmade world
Sew treasures from scraps

First published April 2017 by
Meteoor Books, Antwerpen, Belgium
www.meteoorbooks.com
www.allsewingpatterns.net
hello@meteoorbooks.com

Text and images
© 2017 Meteoor Books and Giovanna Monfeli
Photography and illustrations by Giovanna Monfeli
Layout by Evelien Degeyter
Printed and bound by Spektar, Bulgaria

ISBN 9789491643156
D/2017/13.030/2

A catalogue record for this book is available from the Royal Library of Belgium.